The Quick AIR FRYER COOKBOOK for Beginners UK

1900 Days Easy, Delicious & Energy-Saving Recipes Book with Step-by-Step Instructions for Perfect Results Every Time

Silhujivija Ruktupavina

Copyright© 2024 By Silhujivija Ruktupavina

All rights reserved worldwide.
No part of this book may be reproduced or transmitted in any form or by any means, electronic or mechanical, including photo- copying, recording or by any information storage and retrieval system, without written permission from the publisher, except for the inclusion of brief quotations in a review.

Warning-Disclaimer
The purpose of this book is to educate and entertain. The author or publisher does not guarantee that anyone following the techniques, suggestions, tips, ideas, or strategies will become successful. The author and publisher shall have neither liability or responsibility to anyone with respect to any loss or damage caused, or alleged to be caused, directly or indirectly by the information contained in this book.

TABLE OF CONTENTS

1	Introduction	
5	Chapter 1	Breakfasts
13	Chapter 2	Family Favorites
17	Chapter 3	Fast and Easy Everyday Favourites
21	Chapter 4	Poultry
31	Chapter 5	Fish and Seafood
41	Chapter 6	Beef, Pork, and Lamb
51	Chapter 7	Snacks and Starters
59	Chapter 8	Vegetables and Sides
65	Chapter 9	Vegetarian Mains
69	Chapter 10	Desserts
73	Appendix 1:	Basic Kitchen Conversions & Equivalents
74	Appendix 2:	Recipes Index

INTRODUCTION

Cooking has always been at the heart of human connection, bringing families and friends together over shared meals and cherished recipes. Yet, in today's fast-paced world, where time often feels like a luxury, many of us are seeking ways to simplify cooking without sacrificing flavor, health, or creativity. Enter the air fryer: a revolutionary kitchen appliance that has transformed how we think about food preparation. Whether you are a seasoned chef, a home cook, or someone just starting their culinary journey, the air fryer offers something for everyone. This book is your comprehensive guide to unlocking the full potential of this versatile tool, and in this introduction, we'll explore why the air fryer deserves a permanent spot on your kitchen counter.

The Air Fryer Phenomenon: From Trend to Kitchen Staple

The air fryer has quickly risen from a niche gadget to a must-have appliance, winning over millions of households across the globe. But what is it about the air fryer that has made it so popular? At first glance, it might seem like just another device promising convenience, but it's so much more than that. The air fryer uses rapid air circulation and high temperatures to mimic the effects of frying, baking, and roasting, all while using a fraction of the oil required for traditional methods. The result is food that's crispy on the outside, tender on the inside, and incredibly flavorful—without the guilt of excessive oil consumption.

This revolutionary technology has made it possible for anyone to recreate their favorite fried foods in a healthier way. Imagine enjoying golden, crunchy French fries or perfectly crispy chicken wings without the heavy feeling that often accompanies deep-fried dishes. But the air fryer isn't just for frying. Its versatility allows you to bake fluffy muffins, roast caramelized vegetables, grill juicy steaks, and even reheat leftovers to taste as good as the day they were made. This adaptability has cemented its place as a go-to appliance for busy families, health enthusiasts, and foodies alike.

What truly sets the air fryer apart is its ability to bridge the gap between indulgence and nutrition. Unlike traditional cooking methods that can strip food of its nutrients or require unhealthy amounts of fat, the air fryer preserves the natural flavors and textures of ingredients while enhancing their appeal. It's no wonder that the air fryer has become synonymous with convenience, health, and culinary creativity.

Healthier Meals Without Compromising Flavor

One of the most compelling reasons to invest in an air fryer is the opportunity to create healthier meals without sacrificing flavor. Traditional frying methods require food to be submerged in oil, which significantly increases calorie and fat content. For those looking to reduce their oil intake, this can feel like a trade-off between health and taste. However, the air fryer offers a game-changing solution: you can achieve the same crispy, golden-brown texture and rich flavor with little to no oil.

The air fryer's health benefits extend beyond oil reduction. It encourages the use of fresh, wholesome ingredients, allowing you to focus on creating balanced, nutrient-rich dishes. Vegetables roasted in an air fryer retain their vibrant colors and natural sweetness, making them irresistible even to the pickiest eaters. Proteins such as chicken, fish, and tofu emerge perfectly cooked, with a crispy exterior and juicy interior. Even traditionally indulgent treats like onion rings, mozzarella sticks, and donuts can be reimagined in the air fryer, giving you all the satisfaction with far fewer calories.

For those with dietary restrictions or specific health goals, the air fryer is an invaluable tool. Whether you're following a low-carb, gluten-free, or plant-based diet, the air fryer makes it easy to adapt recipes to suit your needs. This cookbook is packed with recipes that cater to a wide range of preferences, ensuring that everyone at your table can enjoy a delicious and satisfying meal.

Convenience Meets Creativity: Transforming Everyday Cooking

In addition to its health benefits, the air fryer shines as a beacon of convenience. Life can be hectic, and the last thing most of us want after a long day is to spend hours in the kitchen. With the air fryer, cooking becomes quicker, easier, and more enjoyable. Its intuitive design and straightforward operation make it accessible to cooks of all skill levels. Simply season your ingredients, place them in the basket, set the timer, and let the air fryer work its magic.

One of the standout features of the air fryer is its speed. Cooking times are often cut in half compared to traditional methods, making it possible to prepare a wholesome meal in under 30 minutes. Need a quick breakfast? Whip up crispy bacon and eggs in minutes. Planning a weeknight dinner? The air fryer can handle everything from salmon fillets to stuffed peppers with ease. Hosting a party? Impress your guests with bite-sized appetizers like mini quiches or buffalo cauliflower bites.

And the best part? Cleanup is a breeze. Most air fryer components are non-stick and dishwasher-safe, meaning you can spend more time enjoying your meal and less time scrubbing pots and pans. This combination of speed, simplicity, and minimal cleanup makes the air fryer an indispensable tool for modern kitchens.

But convenience doesn't mean sacrificing creativity. The air fryer opens up a world of culinary possibilities, encouraging you to experiment with flavors, textures, and ingredients. From classic comfort foods to adventurous global dishes, the recipes in this book are designed to inspire and delight. You'll learn how to make everything from crispy sweet potato fries and tender ribs to decadent desserts like lava cakes and churros. No matter your taste preferences, the air fryer empowers you to create restaurant-quality dishes at home.

Your Journey Starts Here: Embrace the Air Fryer Lifestyle

The air fryer is more than just a kitchen appliance—it's a gateway to a healthier, more convenient, and more enjoyable way of cooking. It's about reclaiming time, enhancing flavor, and making meals that nourish both body and soul. Whether you're a busy professional, a parent juggling multiple responsibilities, or someone eager to explore new culinary horizons, the air fryer is your ally in the kitchen.

This cookbook is your ultimate guide to mastering the art of air frying. Within these pages, you'll find a wide variety of recipes, tips, and techniques designed to help you make the most of your air fryer. From quick snacks to elaborate feasts, every recipe has been crafted with care to ensure maximum flavor and satisfaction. We'll also share troubleshooting tips and practical advice to ensure your air fryer journey is smooth and successful.

So, are you ready to join the air fryer revolution? Let's embark on this delicious adventure together. With this book as your guide, you'll not only discover the endless possibilities of air frying but also fall in love with cooking all over again. The road to healthier, tastier, and easier meals starts here—let's take the first step.

Chapter 1

Breakfasts

Chapter 1 Breakfasts

Italian Egg Cups

Prep time: 5 minutes | Cook time: 10 minutes | Serves 4

- rapeseed oil
- 235 ml marinara sauce
- 4 eggs
- 4 tablespoons grated Cheddar cheese
- 4 teaspoons grated Parmesan cheese
- Salt and freshly ground black pepper, to taste
- Chopped fresh basil, for garnish

1. Coat four small ramekins lightly with rapeseed oil spray. 2. Divide 60 ml of marinara sauce evenly into the bottom of each ramekin. 3. Carefully break an egg into each ramekin, letting it rest gently on the marinara layer. 4. Sprinkle each egg with 1 tablespoon of shredded Mozzarella and 1 tablespoon of grated Parmesan cheese, then season lightly with salt and pepper. 5. Tightly cover the ramekins with aluminium foil and arrange two of them in the basket of an air fryer. 6. Cook the covered ramekins in the air fryer at 180°C for 5 minutes, then remove the foil and continue cooking until the cheese is golden and the egg whites are set, about 2 to 4 minutes more. For firmer yolks, extend the cooking time by 3 to 5 minutes. 7. Repeat the same process with the remaining ramekins, garnish each serving with fresh basil, and enjoy immediately.

Golden Banana Walnut Loaf

Prep time: 10 minutes | Cook time: 23 minutes | Serves 6

- rapeseed oil cooking spray
- 2 ripe medium bananas
- 1 large egg
- 60 ml non-fat natural yoghurt
- 60 ml rapeseed oil
- ½ teaspoon vanilla extract
- 2 tablespoons honey
- 120 g wholemeal flour
- ¼ teaspoon salt
- ¼ teaspoon baking soda
- ½ teaspoon ground cinnamon
- 60 g chopped walnuts

1. Preheat the air fryer to 180°C. Lightly coat the inside of a 8-by-4-inch loaf pan with rapeseed oil cooking spray. (Or use two 5 ½-by-3-inch loaf pans.) 2. In a large bowl, mash the bananas with a fork. Add the egg, yoghurt, rapeseed oil, vanilla, and honey. Mix until well combined and mostly smooth. 3. Sift the wholemeal flour, salt, baking soda, and cinnamon into the wet mixture, then stir until just combined. Do not overmix. 4. Gently fold in the walnuts. 5. Pour into the prepared loaf pan and spread to distribute evenly. 6. Place the loaf pan in the air fryer basket and bake for 20 to 23 minutes, or until golden brown on top and a toothpick inserted into the center comes out clean. 7. Allow to cool for 5 minutes before serving.

Berry Bliss Breakfast Tarts

Prep time: 15 minutes | Cook time: 10 minutes | Serves 6

- 2 refrigerated piecrusts
- 120 g strawberry preserves
- 1 teaspoon cornflour
- Cooking oil spray
- 120 ml low-fat vanilla yoghurt
- 30 g soft cheese, at room temperature
- 3 tablespoons icing sugar
- Rainbow sprinkles, for decorating

1. Place the piecrusts on a flat surface. Using a knife or pizza cutter, cut each piecrust into 3 rectangles, for 6 total. Discard any unused dough from the piecrust edges. 2. In a small bowl, stir together the preserves and cornflour. Mix well, ensuring there are no lumps of cornflour remaining. 3. Scoop 1 tablespoon of the strawberry mixture onto the top half of each piece of piecrust. 4. Fold the bottom of each piece up to enclose the filling. Using the back of a fork, press along the edges of each tart to seal. 5. Insert the crisper plate into the basket and the basket into the unit. Preheat the unit by selecting BAKE, setting the temperature to 190°C, and setting the time to 3 minutes. Select START/STOP to begin. 6. Once the unit is preheated, spray the crisper plate with cooking oil. Working in batches, spray the breakfast tarts with cooking oil and place them into the basket in a single layer. Do not stack the tarts. 7. Select BAKE, set the temperature to 190°C, and set the time to 10 minutes. Select START/STOP to begin. 8. When the cooking is complete, the tarts should be light golden brown. Let the breakfast tarts cool fully before removing them from the basket. 9. Repeat steps 5, 6, 7, and 8 for the remaining breakfast tarts. 10. In a small bowl, stir together the yoghurt, soft cheese, and icing sugar. Spread the breakfast tarts with the frosting and top with sprinkles.

Golden Banana Walnut Muffins

Prep time: 5 minutes | Cook time: 15 minutes | Makes 10 muffins

- Oil, for spraying
- 2 very ripe bananas
- 95 g packed light soft brown sugar
- 80 ml rapeseed oil or vegetable oil
- 1 large egg
- 1 teaspoon vanilla extract
- 90 g plain flour
- 1 teaspoon baking powder
- 1 teaspoon ground cinnamon
- 120 g chopped walnuts

1. Preheat the air fryer to 160°C. Spray 10 silicone muffin cups lightly with oil. 2. In a medium bowl, mash the bananas. Add the soft brown sugar, rapeseed oil, egg, and vanilla and stir to combine. 3. Fold in the flour, baking powder, and cinnamon until just combined. 4. Add the walnuts and fold a few times to distribute throughout the batter. 5. Divide the batter equally among the prepared muffin cups and place them in the basket. You may need to work in batches, depending on the size of your air fryer. 6. Cook for 15 minutes, or until golden brown and a toothpick inserted into the center of a muffin comes out clean. The air fryer tends to brown muffins more than the oven, so don't be alarmed if they are darker than you're used to. They will still taste great. 7. Let cool on a wire rack before serving.

Lemon-Blueberry Muffins

Prep time: 5 minutes | Cook time: 20 to 25 minutes | Makes 6 muffins

- 150 g almond flour
- 3 tablespoons granulated sweetener
- 1 teaspoon baking powder
- 2 large eggs
- 3 tablespoons melted butter
- 1 tablespoon almond milk
- 1 tablespoon fresh lemon juice
- 120 g fresh blueberries

1. Preheat the air fryer to 180°C and lightly grease 6 silicone muffin cups with vegetable oil, ensuring even coverage. Set the prepared cups aside.2. In a large bowl, mix together the almond flour, sweetener, and baking soda until evenly combined. Set the dry mixture aside.3. In a smaller bowl, whisk the eggs, melted butter, milk, and lemon juice until fully blended. Pour the wet ingredients into the dry mixture and stir gently until just combined. Carefully fold in the blueberries and let the batter rest for 5 minutes to thicken.4. Divide the batter evenly among the greased muffin cups, filling each about two-thirds full. Arrange the cups in the air fryer basket, ensuring space for air circulation.5. Bake the muffins in the air fryer for 20 to 25 minutes, or until a toothpick inserted into the center comes out clean. The tops should be golden brown and firm to the touch.6. Carefully remove the basket from the air fryer and allow the muffins to cool in the cups for 5 minutes. Transfer the muffins to a wire rack to cool completely before serving or storing. Enjoy fresh!

Cheesy Spinach Delight Omelet

Prep time: 5 minutes | Cook time: 12 minutes | Serves 2

- 4 large eggs
- 350 g chopped fresh spinach leaves
- 2 tablespoons peeled and chopped brown onion
- 2 tablespoons salted butter, melted
- 120 g grated mild Cheddar cheese
- ¼ teaspoon salt

1. In an ungreased round nonstick baking dish, whisk eggs. Stir in spinach, onion, butter, Cheddar, and salt. 2. Place dish into air fryer basket. Adjust the temperature to 160°C and bake for 12 minutes. Omelet will be done when browned on the top and firm in the middle. 3. Slice in half and serve warm on two medium plates.

Quick and Easy Blueberry Muffins

Prep time: 10 minutes | Cook time: 12 minutes | Makes 8 muffins

- 160 g flour
- 96 g sugar
- 2 teaspoons baking powder
- ¼ teaspoon salt
- 80 ml rapeseed oil
- 1 egg
- 120 ml milk
- 160 g blueberries, fresh or frozen and thawed

1. Begin by preheating the air fryer to 170°C to ensure consistent baking.2. In a medium-sized mixing bowl, whisk together the flour, sugar, baking powder, and salt until well combined.3. In a separate bowl, mix the oil, egg, and milk thoroughly until the wet ingredients are fully blended.4. Gradually add the wet mixture to the dry ingredients, stirring gently until just combined. Avoid overmixing to keep the batter light.5. Carefully fold in the blueberries, ensuring they are evenly distributed throughout the batter.6. Line muffin cups with parchment paper and spoon the batter evenly into each cup, filling them about three-quarters full.7. Place 4 muffin cups into the air fryer basket, making sure they are spaced apart for proper air circulation. Bake for 12 minutes, or until the tops spring back when gently pressed.8. Remove the first batch and repeat the baking process with the remaining muffin cups.9. Serve the muffins warm for the best texture and flavor. Enjoy immediately!

Bacon, Egg, and Cheese Roll Ups

Prep time: 15 minutes | Cook time: 15 minutes | Serves 4

- 2 tablespoons unsalted butter
- 60 g chopped onion
- ½ medium green pepper, seeded and chopped
- 6 large eggs
- 12 slices bacon
- 235 g grated mature Cheddar cheese
- 120 ml mild tomato salsa, for dipping

1. Heat butter in a medium frying pan over medium heat. Add diced onions and peppers, cooking for about 3 minutes until the onions turn translucent and the mixture becomes aromatic.2. In a small bowl, whisk the eggs thoroughly, then pour them into the frying pan. Stir constantly, scrambling the eggs with the sautéed onions and peppers until they are fluffy and fully cooked, which takes about 5 minutes. Remove the pan from heat and set the scrambled eggs aside.3. On a flat surface, arrange three slices of bacon side by side, overlapping them slightly by about ¼ inch. Spoon 60 ml of the scrambled egg mixture onto the end closest to you, then sprinkle 60 ml of shredded cheese evenly over the eggs.4. Roll the bacon tightly around the egg mixture, starting from the filled end, and secure the seam with a toothpick if needed. Repeat for all rolls and place them into the air fryer basket with enough space to allow for even cooking.5. Set the air fryer temperature to 180°C and cook the rolls for 15 minutes. Halfway through cooking, turn the rolls to ensure even browning and crispiness.6. Once the bacon is golden brown and crispy, remove the rolls from the air fryer. Serve immediately with tomato salsa on the side for dipping and enjoy!

Herbed Sunrise Pitta

Prep time: 5 minutes | Cook time: 6 minutes | Serves 2

- 1 wholemeal pitta
- 2 teaspoons rapeseed oil
- ½ shallot, diced
- ¼ teaspoon garlic, minced
- 1 large egg
- ¼ teaspoon dried oregano
- ¼ teaspoon dried thyme
- ⅛ teaspoon salt
- 2 tablespoons grated Parmesan cheese

1. Preheat the air fryer to 190°C. 2. Brush the top of the pitta with rapeseed oil, then spread the diced shallot and minced garlic over the pitta. 3. Crack the egg into a small bowl or ramekin, and season it with oregano, thyme, and salt. 4. Place the pitta into the air fryer basket, and gently pour the egg onto the top of the pitta. Sprinkle with cheese over the top. 5. Bake for 6 minutes. 6. Allow to cool for 5 minutes before cutting into pieces for serving.

Easy Banger Pizza

Prep time: 10 minutes | Cook time: 6 minutes | Serves 4

- 2 tablespoons ketchup
- 1 pitta bread
- 80 g banger meat
- 230 g Cheddar cheese
- 1 teaspoon garlic powder
- 1 tablespoon rapeseed oil

1. Set the air fryer to preheat at 170°C to prepare for even cooking.2. Evenly spread a thin layer of ketchup across the surface of the pitta bread, ensuring full coverage.3. Add the banger meat as a topping, followed by a generous layer of shredded cheese. Lightly sprinkle garlic powder over the top, then drizzle with a small amount of rapeseed oil for added flavor and crispiness.4. Carefully place the assembled pitta pizza into the air fryer basket, ensuring it lies flat. Cook for 6 minutes, or until the cheese is melted and bubbly, and the edges are lightly crisped.5. Remove from the air fryer and serve immediately while warm for a simple and satisfying meal.

Mixed Berry Bliss Muffins

Prep time: 15 minutes | Cook time: 12 to 17 minutes | Makes 8 muffins

- 160 g plus 1 tablespoon plain flour, divided
- 48 g granulated sugar
- 2 tablespoons light soft brown sugar
- 2 teaspoons baking powder
- 2 eggs
- 160 ml whole milk
- 80 ml neutral oil
- 235 g mixed fresh berries

1. In a medium bowl, stir together 315 g of flour, the granulated sugar, soft brown sugar, and baking powder until mixed well. 2. In a small bowl, whisk the eggs, milk, and oil until combined. Stir the egg mixture into the dry ingredients just until combined. 3. In another small bowl, toss the mixed berries with the remaining 1 tablespoon of flour until coated. Gently stir the berries into the batter. 4. Double up 16 foil muffin cups to make 8 cups. 5. Insert the crisper plate into the basket and the basket into the unit. Preheat the unit by selecting BAKE, setting the temperature to 160°C, and setting the time to 3 minutes. Select START/STOP to begin. 6. Once the unit is preheated, place 1 L into the basket and fill each three-quarters full with the batter. 7. Select BAKE, set the temperature to 160°C, and set the time for 17 minutes. Select START/STOP to begin. 8. After about 12 minutes, check the muffins. If they spring back when lightly touched with your finger, they are done. If not, resume cooking. 9. When the cooking is done, transfer the muffins to a wire rack to cool. 10. Repeat steps 6, 7, and 8 with the remaining muffin cups and batter. 11. Let the muffins cool for 10 minutes before serving.

Bacon & Egg Breakfast Cups

Prep time: 5 minutes | Cook time: 15 minutes | Serves 1

- 2 eggs
- 110 g bacon, cooked
- Salt and ground black pepper, to taste

1. Preheat the air fryer to 200ºC. Put liners in a regular cupcake tin. 2. Crack an egg into each of the cups and add the bacon. Season with some pepper and salt. 3. Bake in the preheated air fryer for 15 minutes, or until the eggs are set. Serve warm.

Almond Bliss Pancakes

Prep time: 5 minutes | Cook time: 30 minutes | Serves 2

- 120 g blanched finely ground almond flour
- 2 tablespoons granular erythritol
- 1 tablespoon salted butter, melted
- 1 large egg
- 80 ml unsweetened almond milk
- ½ teaspoon vanilla extract

1. In a large bowl, mix all ingredients together, then pour half the batter into an ungreased round nonstick baking dish. 2. Place dish into air fryer basket. Adjust the temperature to 160ºC and bake for 15 minutes. The pancake will be golden brown on top and firm, and a toothpick inserted in the center will come out clean when done. Repeat with remaining batter. 3. Slice in half in dish and serve warm.

Strawberry Toast

Prep time: 10 minutes | Cook time: 8 minutes | Makes 4 toasts

- 4 slices bread, ½-inch thick
- Butter-flavoured cooking spray
- 235 g sliced strawberries
- 1 teaspoon sugar

1. Coat one side of each slice of bread generously with butter-flavored cooking spray and place them sprayed side down on a clean surface. 2. Evenly distribute the sliced strawberries across the unsprayed side of the bread slices, ensuring they are spread out but still cover most of the surface. 3. Sprinkle the strawberries with an even layer of sugar to create a sweet and glossy finish during cooking. Arrange the prepared slices in a single layer inside the air fryer basket, ensuring they do not overlap. 4. Set the air fryer to 200ºC and cook for 8 minutes, allowing the bottoms to become golden and crispy while the tops achieve a shiny, caramelized glaze. Serve immediately for the best texture and flavor.

Onion Omelette

Prep time: 10 minutes | Cook time: 12 minutes | Serves 2

- 3 eggs
- Salt and ground black pepper, to taste
- ½ teaspoons soy sauce
- 1 large onion, chopped
- 2 tablespoons grated Cheddar cheese
- Cooking spray

1. Set the air fryer to 180ºC to preheat, ensuring it reaches the ideal temperature for even cooking. 2. In a mixing bowl, whisk together the eggs, salt, pepper, and soy sauce until well combined and slightly frothy. 3. Lightly coat a small oven-safe pan with cooking spray, then evenly distribute the chopped onion across the base of the pan. Place the pan into the preheated air fryer and cook for 6 minutes, allowing the onion to soften and turn translucent. 4. Pour the egg mixture over the onions, ensuring they are evenly coated. Sprinkle the shredded cheese over the top, creating a cheesy layer, and return the pan to the air fryer. Bake for an additional 6 minutes, or until the eggs are set and the cheese is melted. 5. Let the dish cool slightly before serving to allow the flavors to meld and the texture to stabilize. Enjoy as a simple and flavorful meal or snack.

Savory Spinach & Swiss Mushroom Frittata

Prep time: 10 minutes | Cook time: 20 minutes | Serves 4

- rapeseed oil cooking spray
- 8 large eggs
- ½ teaspoon salt
- ½ teaspoon black pepper
- 1 garlic clove, minced
- 475 g fresh baby spinach
- 110 g baby mushrooms, sliced
- 1 shallot, diced
- 120 g grated Swiss cheese, divided
- Hot sauce, for serving (optional)

1. Preheat the air fryer to 180ºC. Lightly coat the inside of a 6-inch round cake pan with rapeseed oil cooking spray. 2. In a large bowl, beat the eggs, salt, pepper, and garlic for 1 to 2 minutes, or until well combined. 3. Fold in the spinach, mushrooms, shallot, and 60 ml the Swiss cheese. 4. Pour the egg mixture into the prepared cake pan, and sprinkle the remaining 60 ml Swiss over the top. 5. Place into the air fryer and bake for 18 to 20 minutes, or until the eggs are set in the center. 6. Remove from the air fryer and allow to cool for 5 minutes. Drizzle with hot sauce (if using) before serving.

Spinach and Bacon Roll-ups

Prep time: 5 minutes | Cook time: 8 to 9 minutes | Serves 4

- 4 wheat maize wraps (6- or 7-inch size)
- 4 slices Swiss cheese
- 235 g baby spinach leaves
- 4 slices turkey bacon
- Special Equipment:
- 4 cocktail sticks, soak in water for at least 30 minutes

1. Begin by preheating the air fryer to 200°C to prepare for quick and even cooking. 2. Lay each tortilla flat on a clean work surface. Place a slice of cheese in the center of each tortilla and evenly distribute 60 ml of fresh spinach on top. Roll each tortilla tightly into a compact cylinder. 3. Wrap a strip of turkey bacon around each rolled tortilla, securing it in place with a toothpick to hold its shape during cooking. 4. Place the prepared roll-ups into the air fryer basket, ensuring they are spaced apart to allow air circulation for even crisping. 5. Cook the roll-ups in the air fryer for 4 minutes, then use tongs to flip and rearrange them for balanced cooking. Continue air frying for an additional 4 to 5 minutes, or until the bacon is golden and crispy. 6. Let the roll-ups rest for 5 minutes after cooking to cool slightly. Carefully remove the toothpicks before serving for a delicious and easy-to-handle snack or appetizer.

Golden Melt Breakfast Quesadillas

Prep time: 10 minutes | Cook time: 15 minutes | Serves 4

- 4 eggs
- 2 tablespoons skimmed milk
- Salt and pepper, to taste
- Oil for misting or cooking spray
- 4 wheat maize wraps
- 4 tablespoons tomato salsa
- 60 g Cheddar cheese, grated
- ½ small avocado, peeled and thinly sliced

1. Preheat the air fryer to 130°C. 2. Beat together eggs, milk, salt, and pepper. 3. Spray a baking pan lightly with cooking spray and add egg mixture. 4. Bake for 8 to 9 minutes, stirring every 1 to 2 minutes, until eggs are scrambled to your liking. Remove and set aside. 5. Spray one side of each maize wrap with oil or cooking spray. Flip over. 6. Divide eggs, tomato salsa, cheese, and avocado among the maize wraps, covering only half of each maize wrap. 7. Fold each maize wrap in half and press down lightly. 8. Place 2 maize wraps in air fryer basket and air fry at 200°C for 3 minutes or until cheese melts and outside feels slightly crispy. Repeat with remaining two maize wraps. 9. Cut each cooked maize wrap into halves or thirds.

Herbed Turkey Apple Patties

Prep time: 5 minutes | Cook time: 10 minutes | Serves 4

- 1 tablespoon chopped fresh thyme
- 1 tablespoon chopped fresh sage
- 1¼ teaspoons coarse or flaky salt
- 1 teaspoon chopped fennel seeds
- ¾ teaspoon smoked paprika
- ½ teaspoon onion granules
- ½ teaspoon garlic powder
- ⅛ teaspoon crushed red pepper flakes
- ⅛ teaspoon freshly ground black pepper
- 450 g lean turkey mince
- 120 g finely minced sweet apple (peeled)

1. Thoroughly combine the thyme, sage, salt, fennel seeds, paprika, onion granules, garlic powder, red pepper flakes, and black pepper in a medium bowl. 2. Add the turkey mince and apple and stir until well incorporated. Divide the mixture into 8 equal portions and shape into patties with your hands, each about ¼ inch thick and 3 inches in diameter. 3. Preheat the air fryer to 200°C. 4. Place the patties in the air fryer basket in a single layer. You may need to work in batches to avoid overcrowding. 5. Air fry for 5 minutes. Flip the patties and air fry for 5 minutes, or until the patties are nicely browned and cooked through. 6. Remove from the basket to a plate and repeat with the remaining patties. 7. Serve warm.

Airy Delight Toaster Treats

Prep time: 10 minutes | Cook time: 11 minutes | Makes 6 pastries

- Oil, for spraying
- 1 (425 g) package ready-to-roll pie crust
- 6 tablespoons jam or preserves of choice
- 340 g icing sugar
- 3 tablespoons milk
- 1 to 2 tablespoons sprinkles of choice

1. Preheat the air fryer to 180°C. Line the air fryer basket with parchment and lightly spray with oil. 2. Cut the pie crust into 12 rectangles, about 3 by 4 inches each. You will need to reroll the dough scraps to get 12 rectangles. 3. Spread 1 tablespoon of jam in the centre of 6 rectangles, leaving ¼ inch around the edges. 4. Pour some water into a small bowl. Use your finger to moisten the edge of each rectangle. 5. Top each rectangle with another and use your fingers to press around the edges. Using the prongs of a fork, seal the edges of the dough and poke a few holes in the top of each one. Place the pastries in the prepared basket. 6. Air fry for 11 minutes. Let cool completely. 7. In a medium bowl, whisk together the icing sugar and milk. Spread the icing over the tops of the pastries and add sprinkles. Serve immediately.

Bacon-and-Eggs Avocado

Prep time: 5 minutes | Cook time: 17 minutes | Serves 1

- 1 large egg
- 1 avocado, halved, peeled, and pitted
- 2 slices bacon
- Fresh parsley, for serving (optional)
- Sea salt flakes, for garnish (optional)

1. Lightly coat the air fryer basket with avocado oil spray and preheat the air fryer to 160°C. Prepare a small bowl with cold water to cool the egg after cooking.2. For the soft-boiled egg, place it directly in the preheated air fryer basket. Cook for 6 minutes for a soft yolk or 7 minutes for a firmer yolk. Immediately transfer the egg to the cold water bowl and let it cool for 2 minutes. Carefully peel the egg and set it aside.3. Hollow out the centers of the avocado halves with a spoon, creating enough space to snugly fit the soft-boiled egg. Nestle the egg into the cavity of one avocado half and cover it with the other half, reassembling the avocado to look whole.4. Starting from one end, wrap the entire avocado in strips of bacon, ensuring full coverage. Secure the bacon with cocktail sticks to keep it in place during cooking.5. Place the bacon-wrapped avocado in the air fryer basket. Cook for 5 minutes, then flip and cook for an additional 5 minutes, or until the bacon reaches your desired level of crispiness.6. Serve immediately, garnished with fresh parsley and a sprinkle of salt flakes if desired. Store leftovers in an airtight container in the fridge for up to 4 days. To reheat, place in a preheated air fryer at 160°C for 4 minutes or until warmed through. Enjoy!

Sirloin Steaks with Eggs

Prep time: 8 minutes | Cook time: 14 minutes per batch | Serves 4

- Cooking oil spray
- 4 (110 g) sirloin steaks
- 1 teaspoon granulated garlic, divided
- 1 teaspoon salt, divided
- 1 teaspoon freshly ground black pepper, divided
- 4 eggs
- ½ teaspoon paprika

1. Attach the crisper plate securely into the air fryer basket and insert the basket into the unit. Begin preheating by choosing AIR FRY, setting the temperature to 180°C, and the timer to 3 minutes. Press START/STOP to initiate preheating.2. Once preheated, coat the crisper plate lightly with cooking oil. Lay 2 steaks directly onto the crisper plate without adding oil or seasoning at this stage.3. Select AIR FRY again, keeping the temperature at 180°C, and set the timer for 9 minutes. Press START/STOP to begin cooking.4. At the 5-minute mark, open the basket and flip the steaks. Sprinkle each steak with ¼ teaspoon of granulated garlic, ¼ teaspoon of salt, and ¼ teaspoon of pepper. Close the unit and continue cooking until the steaks reach an internal temperature of at least 64°C, ensuring they are cooked properly.5. Once done, transfer the steaks to a plate and cover them loosely with aluminium foil to retain warmth. Repeat the same process with the remaining steaks.6. Lightly grease 4 ramekins with rapeseed oil. Carefully crack an egg into each ramekin, then season the eggs with paprika and the remaining ½ teaspoon of both salt and pepper. Work in batches by placing 2 ramekins into the air fryer basket.7. Select the BAKE function, set the temperature to 170°C, and the timer to 5 minutes. Press START/STOP to cook the eggs.8. Check the eggs for doneness, ensuring they reach an internal temperature of 72°C. Remove the ramekins and repeat the process for the remaining two.9. Plate the cooked eggs alongside the steaks and serve immediately for a delicious meal.

Blueberry Cobbler

Prep time: 5 minutes | Cook time: 15 minutes | Serves 4

- 40 g wholemeal pastry flour
- ¾ teaspoon baking powder
- Dash sea salt
- 120 ml semi-skimmed milk
- 2 tablespoons pure maple syrup
- ½ teaspoon vanilla extract
- Cooking oil spray
- 120 g fresh blueberries
- 60 g muesli

1. In a medium mixing bowl, combine the flour, baking powder, and salt, whisking until evenly blended. Add the milk, maple syrup, and vanilla extract, then gently whisk just until the batter is smooth and well combined. Avoid overmixing.2. Preheat the air fryer by selecting the BAKE function, setting the temperature to 180°C, and the timer to 3 minutes. Press START/STOP to begin the preheating process.3. Lightly spray a 6-by-2-inch round baking pan with cooking oil to prevent sticking. Pour the prepared batter into the pan, spreading it out evenly. Sprinkle the top with blueberries and muesli, distributing them evenly.4. Once the air fryer has finished preheating, carefully place the baking pan into the basket. Ensure it sits level for even cooking.5. Select the BAKE function again, set the temperature to 180°C, and the timer to 15 minutes. Press START/STOP to begin baking.6. When the cooking cycle is complete, check that the cobbler is golden brown and that a knife inserted into the center comes out clean. Let it cool slightly before serving plain or with a dollop of vanilla yogurt for added flavor. Enjoy!

Breakfast Banger and Cauliflower

Prep time: 5 minutes | Cook time: 45 minutes | Serves 4

- 450 g banger meat, cooked and crumbled
- 475 ml double/whipping cream
- 1 head cauliflower, chopped
- 235 g grated Cheddar cheese, plus more for topping
- 8 eggs, beaten
- Salt and ground black pepper, to taste

1. Begin by preheating the air fryer to 180°C to ensure even cooking. 2. In a large mixing bowl, combine the banger sausage, heavy cream, chopped cauliflower, shredded cheese, and beaten eggs. Season generously with salt and ground black pepper, stirring until all ingredients are evenly mixed. 3. Lightly grease a casserole dish and pour the prepared mixture into it, spreading it out evenly. Place the dish into the preheated air fryer and bake for 45 minutes, or until the casserole is firm and cooked through. 4. Once baked, sprinkle additional Cheddar cheese over the top while still hot to let it melt. Serve immediately for a rich and satisfying dish.

Baked Peach Porridge

Prep time: 5 minutes | Cook time: 30 minutes | Serves 6

- rapeseed oil cooking spray
- 475 g certified gluten-free porridge oats
- 475 ml unsweetened almond milk
- 60 ml honey, plus more for drizzling (optional)
- 120 ml non-fat natural yoghurt
- 1 teaspoon vanilla extract
- ½ teaspoon ground cinnamon
- ¼ teaspoon salt
- 350 g diced peaches, divided, plus more for serving (optional)

1. Preheat the air fryer to 190°C and spray the inside of a 6-inch cake pan with rapeseed oil cooking spray to prevent sticking. 2. In a large mixing bowl, combine the oats, almond milk, honey, yoghurt, vanilla extract, cinnamon, and salt, stirring thoroughly until all ingredients are well blended. 3. Gently fold 180 g of diced peaches into the oat mixture, ensuring even distribution. Pour the mixture into the prepared cake pan, spreading it out evenly. 4. Scatter the remaining peaches over the top of the oat mixture for a decorative and flavorful finish. Place the pan into the air fryer and bake for 30 minutes, or until the top is golden and the mixture is set. 5. Remove the pan from the air fryer and let the baked porridge cool for 5 minutes to firm up. Serve warm, garnished with additional fresh fruit and a drizzle of honey if desired, for a wholesome and delicious treat.

Rosemary Sweet Potato Veggie Hash

Prep time: 15 minutes | Cook time: 18 minutes | Serves 6

- 2 medium sweet potatoes, peeled and cut into 1-inch cubes
- ½ green pepper, diced
- ½ red onion, diced
- 110 g baby mushrooms, diced
- 2 tablespoons rapeseed oil
- 1 garlic clove, minced
- ½ teaspoon salt
- ½ teaspoon black pepper
- ½ tablespoon chopped fresh rosemary

1. Preheat the air fryer to 190°C. 2. In a large bowl, toss all ingredients together until the vegetables are well coated and seasonings distributed. 3. Pour the vegetables into the air fryer basket, making sure they are in a single even layer. (If using a smaller air fryer, you may need to do this in two batches.) 4. Roast for 9 minutes, then toss or flip the vegetables. Roast for 9 minutes more. 5. Transfer to a serving bowl or individual plates and enjoy.

Chapter 2

Family Favorites

Chapter 2 Family Favorites

Cajun Shrimp & Veggie Skillet

Prep time: 15 minutes | Cook time: 9 minutes | Serves 4

- Oil, for spraying
- 450 g king prawns, peeled and deveined
- 1 tablespoon Cajun seasoning
- 170 g Polish banger, cut into thick slices
- ½ medium courgette, cut into ¼-inch-thick slices
- ½ medium yellow marrow or butternut marrow, cut into ¼-inch-thick slices
- 1 green pepper, seeded and cut into 1-inch pieces
- 2 tablespoons olive oil
- ½ teaspoon salt

1. Preheat the air fryer to 200ºC. 2. Line the air fryer basket with parchment and spray lightly with oil. In a large bowl, toss together the shrimp and Cajun seasoning. 3. Add the kielbasa, courgette, marrow, pepper, olive oil, and salt and mix well. 4. Transfer the mixture to the prepared basket, taking care not to overcrowd. 5. You may need to work in batches, depending on the size of your air fryer. 6. Cook for 9 minutes, shaking and stirring every 3 minutes. 7. Serve immediately.

Balsamic Steak & Veggie Skewers

Prep time: 15 minutes | Cook time: 5 to 7 minutes | Serves 4

- 2 tablespoons balsamic vinegar
- 2 teaspoons olive oil
- ½ teaspoon dried marjoram
- ⅛ teaspoon ground black pepper
- 340 g silverside, cut into 1-inch pieces
- 1 red pepper, sliced
- 16 button mushrooms
- 235 g cherry tomatoes

1. In a medium bowl, stir together the balsamic vinegar, olive oil, marjoram, and black pepper. 2. Add the steak and stir to coat. Let stand for 10 minutes at room temperature. 3. Alternating items, thread the beef, red pepper, mushrooms, and tomatoes onto 8 bamboo or metal skewers that fit in the air fryer. 4. Air fry at 200ºC for 5 to 7 minutes, or until the beef is browned and reaches at least 64ºC on a meat thermometer. 5. Serve immediately.

Bacon-Wrapped Hot Dogs

Prep time: 5 minutes | Cook time: 10 minutes | Serves 4

- Oil, for spraying
- 4 bacon rashers
- 4 hot dog bangers
- 4 hot dog rolls
- Toppings of choice

1. Line the air fryer basket with parchment paper and lightly spray it with oil to prevent sticking. 2. Wrap each hot dog tightly with a strip of bacon, ensuring the tips are covered to avoid over-crisping. Secure both ends of the bacon with toothpicks to keep it in place during cooking. 3. Arrange the bacon-wrapped hot dogs in the prepared air fryer basket, leaving space between them for proper airflow. 4. Set the air fryer to 190ºC and cook for 8 to 9 minutes, adjusting based on your preferred crispiness. For extra-crispy bacon, increase the temperature to 200ºC and cook for 6 to 8 minutes, checking regularly. 5. Once the hot dogs are done, place each one into a bun and return them to the air fryer. Cook for an additional 1 to 2 minutes, just until the buns are warm and slightly toasted. 6. Remove the hot dogs from the air fryer, add your favorite toppings, and serve immediately for a satisfying meal.

Golden Berry Crumble Delight

Prep time: 10 minutes | Cook time: 11 to 16 minutes | Serves 4

- 120 g chopped fresh strawberries
- 120 g fresh blueberries
- 80 g frozen raspberries
- 1 tablespoon freshly squeezed lemon juice
- 1 tablespoon honey
- 80 g wholemeal plain flour
- 3 tablespoons light muscovado sugar
- 2 tablespoons unsalted butter, melted

1. In a baking pan, combine the strawberries, blueberries, and raspberries. 2. Drizzle with the lemon juice and honey. 3. In a small bowl, mix the pastry flour and brown sugar. 4. Stir in the butter and mix until crumbly. 5. Sprinkle this mixture over the fruit. 6. Bake at 190ºC for 11 to 16 minutes, or until the fruit is tender and bubbly and the topping is golden brown. 7. Serve warm.

Steak Tips and Potatoes

Prep time: 10 minutes | Cook time: 20 minutes | Serves 4

- Oil, for spraying
- 227 g baby potatoes, cut in half
- ½ teaspoon salt
- 450 g steak, cut into ½-inch pieces
- 1 teaspoon Worcester sauce
- 1 teaspoon garlic powder
- ½ teaspoon salt
- ½ teaspoon ground black pepper

1. Line the air fryer basket with parchment paper and lightly coat it with oil to prevent sticking.2. In a microwave-safe bowl, combine the diced potatoes and salt, then add enough water to cover the bottom about ½ inch. Microwave for 7 minutes, or until the potatoes are nearly tender but not fully cooked. Drain thoroughly and set aside.3. In a large mixing bowl, combine the steak pieces, par-cooked potatoes, Worcestershire sauce, minced garlic, additional salt, and black pepper. Toss gently to ensure the ingredients are evenly coated with the seasoning.4. Spread the steak and potato mixture in a single, even layer in the prepared air fryer basket, ensuring good airflow for even cooking.5. Set the air fryer to 200ºC and cook for 12 to 17 minutes. Stir the mixture after 5 to 6 minutes to promote even browning. Adjust cooking time based on the thickness of the steak and your preferred level of doneness.6. Once the steak is cooked to your liking and the potatoes are golden and crisp, remove from the air fryer and serve immediately. Enjoy your hearty and flavorful steak and potato dish!

Fried Green Tomatoes

Prep time: 15 minutes | Cook time: 6 to 8 minutes | Serves 4

- 4 medium green tomatoes
- 50 g plain flour
- 2 egg whites
- 60 ml almond milk
- 235 g ground almonds
- 120 g Japanese breadcrumbs
- 2 teaspoons olive oil
- 1 teaspoon paprika
- 1 clove garlic, minced

1. Wash the tomatoes thoroughly and pat them dry with a clean towel. Slice them into ½-inch thick rounds, discarding the thinner end pieces to ensure even cooking. Spread the flour onto a plate for dredging.2. In a shallow bowl, whisk the egg whites with almond milk until the mixture becomes frothy.3. On a separate plate, mix the chopped almonds, breadcrumbs, olive oil, paprika, and garlic powder, stirring until well combined to form a flavorful coating.4. Coat each tomato slice by first dipping it into the flour, then into the egg white mixture, and finally into the almond mixture, pressing gently to adhere the coating evenly.5. Arrange four coated tomato slices in the air fryer basket, leaving space between them for proper airflow.6. Set the air fryer to 200ºC and cook for 6 to 8 minutes, or until the coating is crisp and golden brown. Check occasionally to prevent overcooking.7. Remove the cooked slices and repeat the process with the remaining tomatoes until all are finished.8. Serve the crispy tomato slices immediately for the best flavor and texture. Enjoy as a delicious appetizer or side dish!

Pecan Rolls

Prep time: 20 minutes | Cook time: 20 to 24 minutes | Makes 12 rolls

- 220 g plain flour, plus more for dusting
- 2 tablespoons caster sugar, plus 60 ml, divided
- 1 teaspoon salt
- 3 tablespoons butter, at room temperature
- 180 ml milk, whole or semi-skimmed
- 40 g packed light muscovado sugar
- 120g chopped pecans, toasted
- 1 to 2 tablespoons oil
- 35g icing sugar (optional)

1. In a large mixing bowl, whisk together the flour, 2 tablespoons of caster sugar, and salt until thoroughly combined.2. Add the butter and milk to the dry ingredients and gently stir until a sticky dough forms. In a small separate bowl, mix the brown sugar and the remaining 60 g of caster sugar until evenly blended.3. Lay a piece of parchment paper on a clean work surface and lightly dust it with flour. Roll out the dough on the floured parchment to a thickness of ¼ inch, creating an even rectangle.4. Spread the sugar mixture evenly across the surface of the rolled dough, then sprinkle the pecans over the sugar layer. Starting from one edge, roll the dough tightly into a log, sealing the ends by pinching them together.5. Slice the rolled dough into 12 equal pieces to form individual rolls. Preheat the air fryer to 160ºC to prepare for baking.6. Line the air fryer basket with parchment paper and lightly spray it with oil. Arrange 6 rolls on the parchment, ensuring they have space to expand slightly. Bake for 5 minutes.7. Flip the rolls carefully and continue baking for an additional 5 to 7 minutes, or until they are golden brown and lightly crisped. Repeat the process with the remaining rolls.8. Dust the baked rolls with icing sugar for a decorative and sweet finish, if desired, and serve immediately. Enjoy your homemade pecan rolls!

Meatball Subs

Prep time: 15 minutes | Cook time: 19 minutes | Serves 6

- Oil, for spraying
- 450 g 15% fat minced beef
- 120 ml Italian breadcrumbs (mixed breadcrumbs, Italian seasoning and salt)
- 1 tablespoon dried minced onion
- 1 tablespoon minced garlic
- 1 large egg
- 1 teaspoon salt
- 1 teaspoon freshly ground black pepper
- 6 sub rolls
- 1 (510 g) jar marinara sauce
- 350 ml shredded Mozzarella cheese

1. Line the air fryer basket with parchment paper and lightly spray it with oil to prevent sticking. 2. In a large mixing bowl, combine the ground beef, bread crumbs, finely chopped onion, minced garlic, egg, salt, and black pepper. Mix thoroughly until evenly combined. Shape the mixture into 18 evenly sized meatballs. 3. Arrange the meatballs in a single layer in the prepared air fryer basket, ensuring they do not touch for even cooking. 4. Set the air fryer to 199°C (390°F) and cook the meatballs for 15 minutes, turning them halfway through for even browning. 5. Once cooked, place 3 meatballs into each hoagie roll. Top each roll with marinara sauce and a generous layer of shredded Mozzarella cheese. 6. Place the assembled hoagie rolls back into the air fryer, cooking at 199°C (390°F) for 3 to 4 minutes, or until the cheese is melted and bubbly. Depending on the size of your air fryer, you may need to work in batches. 7. Serve the meatball hoagies immediately while they're hot and gooey for a hearty and satisfying meal.

Zesty Pork Sliders with Red Cabbage Crunch

Prep time: 20 minutes | Cook time: 7 to 9 minutes | Serves 4

- 120 ml Greek yoghurt
- 2 tablespoons low-salt mustard, divided
- 1 tablespoon lemon juice
- 60 g sliced red cabbage
- 60 g grated carrots
- 450 g lean finely chopped pork
- ½ teaspoon paprika
- 235 g mixed salad leaves
- 2 small tomatoes, sliced
- 8 small low-salt wholemeal sandwich buns, cut in half

1. In a small bowl, combine the yoghurt, 1 tablespoon mustard, lemon juice, cabbage, and carrots; mix and refrigerate. 2. In a medium bowl, combine the pork, remaining 1 tablespoon mustard, and paprika. Form into 8 small patties. Put the sliders into the air fryer basket. 3. Air fry at 200°C for 7 to 9 minutes, or until the sliders register 74°C as tested with a meat thermometer. 4. Assemble the burgers by placing some of the lettuce greens on a bun bottom. 5. Top with a tomato slice, the burgers, and the cabbage mixture. 6. Add the bun top and serve immediately.

Gourmet Cauliflower Crust Pizzas

Prep time: 10 minutes | Cook time: 25 minutes | Serves 2

- 1 (340 g) bag frozen riced cauliflower
- 75 g shredded Mozzarella cheese
- 15 g almond flour
- 20 g Parmesan cheese
- 1 large egg
- ½ teaspoon salt
- 1 teaspoon garlic powder
- 1 teaspoon dried oregano
- 4 tablespoons no-sugar-added marinara sauce, divided
- 110 g fresh Mozzarella, chopped, divided
- 140 g cooked chicken breast, chopped, divided
- 100 g chopped cherry tomatoes, divided
- 5 g fresh baby rocket, divided

1. Preheat the air fryer to 200°C. Cut 4 sheets of parchment paper to fit the basket of the air fryer. Brush with olive oil and set aside. 2. In a large glass bowl, microwave the cauliflower according to package directions. Place the cauliflower on a clean towel, draw up the sides, and squeeze tightly over a sink to remove the excess moisture. Return the cauliflower to the bowl and add the shredded Mozzarella along with the almond flour, Parmesan, egg, salt, garlic powder, and oregano. Stir until thoroughly combined. 3. Divide the dough into two equal portions. Place one piece of dough on the prepared parchment paper and pat gently into a thin, flat disk 7 to 8 inches in diameter. Air fry for 15 minutes until the crust begins to brown. Let cool for 5 minutes. 4. Transfer the parchment paper with the crust on top to a baking sheet. Place a second sheet of parchment paper over the crust. While holding the edges of both sheets together, carefully lift the crust off the baking sheet, flip it, and place it back in the air fryer basket. The new sheet of parchment paper is now on the bottom. Remove the top piece of paper and air fry the crust for another 15 minutes until the top begins to brown. Remove the basket from the air fryer. 5. Spread 2 tablespoons of the marinara sauce on top of the crust, followed by half the fresh Mozzarella, chicken, cherry tomatoes, and rocket. Air fry for 5 to 10 minutes longer, until the cheese is melted and beginning to brown. Remove the pizza from the oven and let it sit for 10 minutes before serving. Repeat with the remaining ingredients to make a second pizza.

Chapter 3

Fast and Easy Everyday Favourites

Chapter 3 Fast and Easy Everyday Favourites

Cheesy Chilli Toast

Prep time: 5 minutes | Cook time: 5 minutes | Serves 1

- 2 tablespoons grated Parmesan cheese
- 2 tablespoons grated Mozzarella cheese
- 2 teaspoons salted butter, at room temperature
- 10 to 15 thin slices serrano chilli or jalapeño
- 2 slices sourdough bread
- ½ teaspoon black pepper

1. Set the air fryer to preheat at 160ºC to ensure even cooking. 2. In a medium bowl, thoroughly mix the Parmesan, Mozzarella, softened butter, and finely chopped chillies until the mixture forms a spreadable paste. 3. Spread the cheese mixture generously on one side of each bread slice, ensuring the layer is thick and even for a gooey texture. 4. Add an extra kick by sprinkling a light dusting of freshly cracked black pepper over the cheese-covered side. 5. Line the air fryer basket with parchment paper for easy cleanup, and place the slices of bread cheese-side up in a single layer, leaving space between slices. 6. Cook the bread in the air fryer for 7 minutes at 160ºC, or until the cheese is fully melted, bubbly, and golden brown around the edges. 7. Remove the slices carefully with tongs and serve immediately as a crispy, cheesy snack or appetizer, optionally garnished with fresh herbs like parsley for added flavor.

Golden Cheesy Potato Patties

Prep time: 5 minutes | Cook time: 10 minutes | Serves 8

- 900 g white potatoes
- 120 g finely chopped spring onions
- ½ teaspoon freshly ground black pepper, or more to taste
- 1 tablespoon fine sea salt
- ½ teaspoon hot paprika
- 475 g shredded Colby or Monterey Jack cheese
- 60 ml rapeseed oil
- 235 g crushed crackers

1. Preheat the air fryer to 180ºC. Boil the potatoes until soft. 2. Dry them off and peel them before mashing thoroughly, leaving no lumps. 3. Combine the mashed potatoes with spring onions, pepper, salt, paprika, and cheese. 4. Mould the mixture into balls with your hands and press with your palm to flatten them into patties. 5. In a shallow dish, combine the rapeseed oil and crushed crackers. 6. Coat the patties in the crumb mixture. 7. Bake the patties for about 10 minutes, in multiple batches if necessary. 8. Serve hot.

Beetroot Salad with Lemon Vinaigrette

Prep time: 10 minutes | Cook time: 12 to 15 minutes | Serves 4

- 6 medium red and golden beetroots, peeled and sliced
- 1 teaspoon olive oil
- ¼ teaspoon rock salt

Vinaigrette:
- 2 teaspoons olive oil
- 2 tablespoons chopped fresh chives
- 120 g crumbled feta cheese
- 2 kg mixed greens
- Cooking spray
- Juice of 1 lemon

1. Begin by preheating the air fryer to 180ºC to ensure it's ready for consistent cooking. 2. Peel and cut the beetroots into bite-sized wedges, then toss them in a large bowl with olive oil and a generous sprinkle of rock salt, ensuring they are evenly coated. 3. Line the air fryer basket with parchment paper and spray it lightly with cooking oil to prevent sticking. Arrange the beetroot wedges in a single layer, ensuring they do not overlap. Cook for 15 to 18 minutes, shaking the basket halfway through, until the beets are tender with slightly crisp edges. 4. While the beets are cooking, prepare the vinaigrette. In a separate large bowl, whisk together olive oil, freshly squeezed lemon juice, finely chopped chives, and a pinch of salt and pepper until emulsified. 5. Once the beets are cooked, transfer them directly into the bowl with the vinaigrette while still warm, tossing gently to coat the beets thoroughly. Let them sit for 5 minutes to absorb the flavors. 6. Arrange a bed of mixed greens on a serving platter or individual plates, spoon the dressed beets on top, and finish with a generous scattering of crumbled feta cheese. Serve immediately for a fresh and vibrant dish.

Basil Lentil-Stuffed Tomatoes with Goat Cheese

Prep time: 10 minutes | Cook time: 15 minutes | Serves 4

- 4 tomatoes
- 120 ml cooked red lentils
- 1 garlic clove, minced
- 1 tablespoon minced red onion
- 4 basil leaves, minced
- ¼ teaspoon salt
- ¼ teaspoon black pepper
- 110 g goat cheese
- 2 tablespoons shredded Parmesan cheese

1. Preheat the air fryer to 192°C. 2. Slice the top off of each tomato. Using a knife and spoon, cut and scoop out half of the flesh inside of the tomato. 3. Place it into a medium bowl. To the bowl with the tomato, add the cooked lentils, garlic, onion, basil, salt, pepper, and goat cheese. Stir until well combined. 4. Spoon the filling into the scooped-out cavity of each of the tomatoes, then top each one with ½ tablespoon of shredded Parmesan cheese. 5. Place the tomatoes in a single layer in the air fryer basket and bake for 15 minutes.

Crispy Chorizo Scotch Eggs

Prep time: 5 minutes | Cook time: 15 to 20 minutes | Makes 4 eggs

- 450 g Mexican chorizo or other seasoned banger meat
- 4 soft-boiled eggs plus 1 raw egg
- 1 tablespoon water
- 120 ml plain flour
- 235 ml panko breadcrumbs
- Cooking spray

1. Divide the chorizo into 4 equal portions. Flatten each portion into a disc. Place a soft-boiled egg in the centre of each disc. Wrap the chorizo around the egg, encasing it completely. Place the encased eggs on a plate and chill for at least 30 minutes. 2.Preheat the air fryer to 182°C. 3.Beat the raw egg with 1 tablespoon of water. Place the flour on a small plate and the panko on a second plate. Working with 1 egg at a time, roll the encased egg in the flour, then dip it in the egg mixture. Dredge the egg in the panko and place on a plate. Repeat with the remaining eggs. 4.Spray the eggs with oil and place in the air fryer basket. Bake for 10 minutes. Turn and bake for an additional 5 to 10 minutes, or until browned and crisp on all sides. 5.Serve immediately.

Buttery Sweet Potatoes

Prep time: 5 minutes | Cook time: 10 minutes | Serves 4

- 2 tablespoons melted butter
- 1 tablespoon light brown sugar
- 2 sweet potatoes, peeled and cut into ½-inch cubes
- Cooking spray

1. Set the air fryer to preheat at 200°C. While preheating, prepare the ingredients for a flavorful coating.2. In a large bowl, combine melted butter, brown sugar, a pinch of cinnamon, and a dash of paprika for a sweet and smoky flavor profile. Stir until the mixture forms a smooth glaze.3. Cut the sweet potatoes into evenly sized wedges or chunks, ensuring they cook uniformly. Toss them in the butter mixture, coating each piece thoroughly for maximum flavor.4. Line the air fryer basket with parchment paper and lightly spray it with oil. Arrange the coated sweet potatoes in a single layer on the parchment, leaving space between pieces for optimal crisping.5. Air fry the sweet potatoes for 6 minutes, then shake the basket to turn the pieces for even cooking. Spray them lightly with more oil and air fry for an additional 6 to 8 minutes, or until they are fork-tender and caramelized around the edges.6. Remove the sweet potatoes from the air fryer and serve immediately. Optionally, garnish with a sprinkle of sea salt, chopped parsley, or a drizzle of honey for added flavor and presentation. Enjoy!

Baked Cheese Sandwich

Prep time: 5 minutes | Cook time: 8 minutes | Serves 2

- 2 tablespoons mayonnaise
- 4 thick slices sourdough bread
- 4 thick slices Brie cheese
- 8 slices hot capicola or prosciutto

1. Preheat the air fryer to 180°C to ensure an even cooking environment for your sandwiches.2. Spread a generous layer of mayonnaise on one side of each bread slice. For added flavor, mix a pinch of garlic powder or paprika into the mayonnaise before spreading.3. Place two slices of bread, mayonnaise-side down, into the air fryer basket. Layer the Brie slices evenly on the bread, followed by the capicola for a rich, savory filling.4. Top with the remaining bread slices, mayonnaise-side up, to complete the sandwiches, pressing them lightly to secure the layers.5. Bake in the air fryer for 8 to 10 minutes, flipping halfway through for even browning. Cook until the bread is golden and crisp, and the Brie is melted and gooey.6. Remove from the air fryer, slice diagonally for presentation, and serve immediately. Optionally, pair with a light salad or a dipping sauce for a complete meal. Enjoy your gourmet grilled sandwich!

Garlic Herb Roasted Vegetables

Prep time: 10 minutes | Cook time: 14 to 18 minutes | Serves 4

- 1 red pepper, sliced
- 1 (230 g) package sliced mushrooms
- 235 g runner beans, cut into 2-inch pieces
- 80 g diced red onion
- 3 garlic cloves, sliced
- 1 teaspoon olive oil
- ½ teaspoon dried basil
- ½ teaspoon dried tarragon

1. Preheat the air fryer to 180°C. 2.In a medium bowl, mix the red pepper, mushrooms, runner beans, red onion, and garlic. 3.Drizzle with the olive oil. Toss to coat. 4.Add the herbs and toss again. Place the vegetables in the air fryer basket. 5.Roast for 14 to 18 minutes, or until tender. 6.Serve immediately.

Crispy Homemade Croutons

Prep time: 5 minutes | Cook time: 8 minutes | Serves 4

- 2 sliced bread
- 1 tablespoon olive oil
- Hot soup, for serving

1. Preheat the air fryer to 200°C. 2.Cut the slices of bread into medium-size chunks. 3.Brush the air fryer basket with the oil. 4.Place the chunks inside and air fry for at least 8 minutes. 5.Serve with hot soup.

Beery and Crunchy Onion Rings

Prep time: 10 minutes | Cook time: 16 minutes | Serves 2 to 4

- 80 g plain flour
- 1 teaspoon paprika
- ½ teaspoon bicarbonate of soda
- 1 teaspoon salt
- ½ teaspoon freshly ground black pepper
- 1 egg, beaten
- 180 ml beer
- 175 g breadcrumbs
- 1 tablespoons olive oil
- 1 large Vidalia or sweet onion, peeled and sliced into ½-inch rings
- Cooking spray

1. Preheat the air fryer to 180°C, ensuring it's ready for crisp frying. Lightly spray the basket with cooking oil for non-stick results.2. In a medium bowl, mix the flour, paprika, bicarbonate of soda, salt, and black pepper thoroughly to create a seasoned coating.3. In a separate bowl, whisk together the egg and beer until fully combined, creating a light and airy batter base.4. Make a well in the center of the dry flour mixture, then pour the egg and beer mixture into the well. Stir until a smooth batter forms, avoiding lumps for even coating.5. On a shallow plate, combine breadcrumbs and olive oil, stirring until the crumbs are slightly moistened for a crunchy finish.6. Dip each onion ring into the batter, ensuring it's fully coated. Shake off any excess batter, then press the onion ring into the breadcrumb mixture. Flip to coat both sides thoroughly, pressing gently to adhere the crumbs.7. Arrange the coated onion rings in a single layer in the air fryer basket, leaving space between them for proper air circulation. Cook in batches if necessary.8. Air fry for 16 minutes, flipping the rings and rotating the bottom ones to the top halfway through cooking for even browning. Continue until the rings are golden brown and crispy.9. Serve the onion rings immediately while hot and crunchy. Pair with your favorite dipping sauces for an irresistible appetizer or snack!

Chapter 4

Poultry

Chapter 4 Poultry

Smoky Chipotle Chicken Drumsticks

Prep time: 15 minutes | Cook time: 20 minutes | Serves 4

- 1 tablespoon tomato paste
- ½ teaspoon chipotle powder
- ¼ teaspoon apple cider vinegar
- ¼ teaspoon garlic powder
- 8 chicken drumsticks
- ½ teaspoon salt
- ⅛ teaspoon ground black pepper

1. In a small bowl, combine tomato paste, chipotle powder, vinegar, and garlic powder. 2. Sprinkle drumsticks with salt and pepper, then place into a large bowl and pour in tomato paste mixture. Toss or stir to evenly coat all drumsticks in mixture. 3. Place drumsticks into ungreased air fryer basket. Adjust the temperature to 200ºC and air fry for 25 minutes, turning drumsticks halfway through cooking. Drumsticks will be dark red with an internal temperature of at least 76ºC when done. Serve warm.

Peanut Butter Chicken Satay

Prep time: 12 minutes | Cook time: 12 to 18 minutes | Serves 4

- 120 g crunchy peanut butter
- 80 ml chicken broth
- 3 tablespoons low-sodium soy sauce
- 2 tablespoons freshly squeezed lemon juice
- 2 garlic cloves, minced
- 2 tablespoons extra-virgin olive oil
- 1 teaspoon curry powder
- 450 g chicken tenders
- Cooking oil spray

1. In a medium mixing bowl, whisk together the peanut butter, chicken broth, soy sauce, lemon juice, minced garlic, olive oil, and curry powder until smooth and creamy.2. Transfer 2 tablespoons of the sauce to a separate small bowl for marinating. Pour the rest of the sauce into a serving bowl and set aside for dipping.3. Add the chicken tenders to the small bowl with the reserved 2 tablespoons of sauce, tossing until well coated. Allow the chicken to marinate for at least 5 minutes to absorb the flavors.4. Prepare the air fryer by inserting the crisper plate into the basket and placing the basket into the unit. Preheat by selecting AIR FRY, setting the temperature to 200ºC, and the timer to 3 minutes. Press START/STOP to begin.5. Thread each chicken tender lengthwise onto a 6-inch bamboo skewer, ensuring the skewer holds the meat securely for even cooking.6. Once the air fryer is preheated, spray the crisper plate lightly with cooking oil. Arrange half of the chicken skewers in a single layer in the basket, ensuring no overlapping.7. Select AIR FRY, set the temperature to 200ºC, and the timer to 9 minutes. Press START/STOP to begin cooking.8. After 6 minutes, check the chicken using a food thermometer. If the internal temperature has reached 76ºC, the chicken is fully cooked. If not, continue cooking for the remaining time.9. Repeat the process for the remaining chicken skewers, ensuring all are cooked evenly.10. Once cooking is complete, serve the chicken skewers immediately alongside the reserved dipping sauce for a flavorful, protein-packed dish. Enjoy!

Crispy Parmesan-Coated Chicken Breasts

Prep time: 30 minutes | Cook time: 12 to 14 minutes | Serves 4

- 450 g boneless, skinless chicken breasts
- 180 ml dill gherkin juice
- 35 g finely ground blanched almond flour
- 70 g finely grated Parmesan cheese
- ½ teaspoon sea salt
- ½ teaspoon freshly ground black pepper
- 2 large eggs
- Avocado oil spray

1. Place the chicken breasts in a zip-top bag or between two pieces of cling film. Using a meat mallet or heavy frying pan, pound the chicken to a uniform ½-inch thickness. 2. Place the chicken in a large bowl with the gherkin juice. Cover and allow to brine in the refrigerator for up to 2 hours. 3. In a shallow dish, combine the almond flour, Parmesan cheese, salt, and pepper. In a separate, shallow bowl, beat the eggs. 4. Drain the chicken and pat it dry with paper towels. Dip in the eggs and then in the flour mixture, making sure to press the coating into the chicken. Spray both sides of the coated breasts with oil. 5. Spray the air fryer basket with oil and put the chicken inside. Set the temperature to 200ºC and air fry for 6 to 7 minutes. 6. Carefully flip the breasts with a spatula. Spray the breasts again with oil and continue cooking for 6 to 7 minutes more, until golden and crispy.

Classic Whole Chicken

Prep time: 5 minutes | Cook time: 50 minutes | Serves 4

- Oil, for spraying
- 1 (1.8 kg) whole chicken, giblets removed
- 1 tablespoon olive oil
- 1 teaspoon paprika
- ½ teaspoon granulated garlic
- ½ teaspoon salt
- ½ teaspoon freshly ground black pepper
- ¼ teaspoon finely chopped fresh parsley, for garnish

1. Begin by lining the air fryer basket with parchment paper and spraying it lightly with oil for a non-stick surface. 2. Pat the chicken dry thoroughly with paper towels to ensure the seasoning adheres properly. Rub it all over with olive oil for an even coating that helps achieve a golden, crispy skin. 3. In a small mixing bowl, combine paprika, garlic powder, salt, and black pepper. Sprinkle the seasoning mixture generously and evenly over the entire chicken, making sure to get into every crevice for maximum flavor. 4. Place the chicken in the air fryer basket breast-side down, allowing the back to cook first for a juicier breast. 5. Set the air fryer to 180°C and cook the chicken for 30 minutes. Carefully flip the chicken using tongs and cook for an additional 20 minutes, or until the thickest part of the chicken registers an internal temperature of 76°C and the juices run clear. 6. Remove the chicken from the air fryer and let it rest for 5 minutes to allow the juices to redistribute. Sprinkle with freshly chopped parsley for a vibrant finish and serve immediately. Enjoy a flavorful, crispy, and tender roast chicken!

Parmesan-Crusted Italian Chicken with Mozzarella Sauce

Prep time: 15 minutes | Cook time: 20 minutes | Serves 4

- 2 large skinless chicken breasts (about 565 g)
- Salt and freshly ground black pepper
- 25 g ground almonds
- 45 g grated Parmesan cheese
- 2 teaspoons Italian seasoning
- 1 egg, lightly beaten
- 1 tablespoon olive oil
- 225 g no-sugar-added marinara sauce
- 4 slices Mozzarella cheese or 110 g shredded Mozzarella

1. Preheat the air fryer to 180°C. 2. Slice the chicken breasts in half horizontally to create 4 thinner chicken breasts. Working with one piece at a time, place the chicken between two pieces of parchment paper and pound with a meat mallet or rolling pin to flatten to an even thickness. Season both sides with salt and freshly ground black pepper. 3. In a large shallow bowl, combine the ground almonds, Parmesan, and Italian seasoning; stir until thoroughly combined. Place the egg in another large shallow bowl. 4. Dip the chicken in the egg, followed by the ground almonds mixture, pressing the mixture firmly into the chicken to create an even coating. 5. Working in batches if necessary, arrange the chicken breasts in a single layer in the air fryer basket and coat both sides lightly with olive oil. Pausing halfway through the cooking time to flip the chicken, air fry for 15 minutes, or until a thermometer inserted into the thickest part registers 76°C. 6. Spoon the marinara sauce over each piece of chicken and top with the Mozzarella cheese. Air fry for an additional 3 to 5 minutes until the cheese is melted.

Thanksgiving Turkey Breast

Prep time: 5 minutes | Cook time: 30 minutes | Serves 4

- 1½ teaspoons fine sea salt
- 1 teaspoon ground black pepper
- 1 teaspoon chopped fresh rosemary leaves
- 1 teaspoon chopped fresh sage
- 1 teaspoon chopped fresh tarragon
- 1 teaspoon chopped fresh thyme leaves
- 1 (900 g) turkey breast
- 3 tablespoons ghee or unsalted butter, melted
- 3 tablespoons Dijon mustard

1. Lightly spray the air fryer basket with avocado oil, then preheat the air fryer to 200°C to ensure it's ready for even cooking. 2. In a small bowl, mix together salt, freshly ground black pepper, and your choice of dried herbs, such as thyme, rosemary, and parsley. Coat the turkey breast generously with the seasoning mixture, pressing it gently to adhere. 3. In another bowl, combine softened ghee with Dijon mustard, stirring until smooth. Using a brush, evenly coat all sides of the seasoned turkey breast with the ghee-Dijon mixture, ensuring a flavorful crust. 4. Place the prepared turkey breast into the air fryer basket, ensuring it sits upright and isn't touching the sides for optimal airflow. Cook at 200°C for 30 minutes, or until a meat thermometer inserted into the thickest part of the turkey registers 76°C. 5. Once cooked, transfer the turkey breast to a cutting board and let it rest for 10 minutes. This allows the juices to redistribute, ensuring moist slices. Carve into ½-inch-thick slices for serving. 6. Store any leftovers in an airtight container in the refrigerator for up to 4 days, or freeze for up to a month. To reheat, place the turkey slices in a preheated air fryer at 180°C for 4 minutes, or until heated through. Enjoy your perfectly cooked turkey, whether fresh or reheated!

Butter and Bacon Chicken

Prep time: 10 minutes | Cook time: 65 minutes | Serves 6

- 1 (1.8 kg) whole chicken
- 2 tablespoons salted butter, softened
- 1 teaspoon dried thyme
- ½ teaspoon garlic powder
- 1 teaspoon salt
- ½ teaspoon ground black pepper
- 6 slices sugar-free bacon

1. Thoroughly pat the chicken dry with paper towels to ensure crispy skin. Rub softened butter generously over all sides of the chicken to lock in moisture and enhance flavor. Sprinkle the chicken evenly with thyme, garlic powder, salt, and black pepper for a well-seasoned base. 2. Place the chicken breast-side up in the air fryer basket, ensuring it sits securely without touching the sides. Lay strips of bacon across the top of the chicken, overlapping slightly. Use toothpicks to hold the bacon in place, creating a flavorful layer that will infuse the chicken as it cooks. 3. Preheat the air fryer to 180°C and cook the chicken for 65 minutes. Halfway through the cooking process, carefully remove the basket and take off the bacon strips. Set them aside to stay crispy, and flip the chicken over to ensure even browning on all sides. 4. Continue air frying the chicken until the skin is golden and crispy, and the internal temperature of the thickest part of the chicken reaches at least 76°C. Use a meat thermometer for accuracy. 5. Once cooked, transfer the chicken to a serving platter and let it rest for 5 minutes to allow the juices to redistribute. Reheat the bacon strips briefly if needed, then serve the chicken warm, accompanied by the crispy bacon for an indulgent, savory meal.

Juicy Air-Fried Turkey Tenderloin

Prep time: 20 minutes | Cook time: 30 minutes | Serves 4

- Olive oil
- ½ teaspoon paprika
- ½ teaspoon garlic powder
- ½ teaspoon salt
- ½ teaspoon freshly ground black pepper
- Pinch cayenne pepper
- 680 g turkey breast tenderloin

1. Spray the air fryer basket lightly with olive oil. 2. In a small bowl, combine the paprika, garlic powder, salt, black pepper, and cayenne pepper. Rub the mixture all over the turkey. 3. Place the turkey in the air fryer basket and lightly spray with olive oil. 4. Air fry at 190°C for 15 minutes. Flip the turkey over and lightly spray with olive oil. Air fry until the internal temperature reaches at least 80°C for an additional 10 to 15 minutes. 5. Let the turkey rest for 10 minutes before slicing and serving.

Curry-Spiced Cranberry Chicken Bowls

Prep time: 12 minutes | Cook time: 18 minutes | Serves 4

- 3 (140 g) low-sodium boneless, skinless chicken breasts, cut into 1½-inch cubes
- 2 teaspoons olive oil
- 2 tablespoons cornflour
- 1 tablespoon curry powder
- 1 tart apple, chopped
- 120 ml low-sodium chicken broth
- 60 g dried cranberries
- 2 tablespoons freshly squeezed orange juice
- Brown rice, cooked (optional)

1. Preheat the air fryer to 196°C. 2. In a medium bowl, mix the chicken and olive oil. Sprinkle with the cornflour and curry powder. Toss to coat. Stir in the apple and transfer to a metal pan. Bake in the air fryer for 8 minutes, stirring once during cooking. 3. Add the chicken broth, cranberries, and orange juice. Bake for about 10 minutes more, or until the sauce is slightly thickened and the chicken reaches an internal temperature of 76°C on a meat thermometer. Serve over hot cooked brown rice, if desired.

Fiesta Lime Chicken Bowl

Prep time: 15 minutes | Cook time: 12 to 15 minutes | Serves 4

- 450 g boneless, skinless chicken breasts (2 large breasts)
- 2 tablespoons lime juice
- 1 teaspoon cumin
- ½ teaspoon salt
- 40 g grated Pepper Jack cheese
- 1 (455 g) tin refried beans
- 130 g salsa
- 30 g shredded lettuce
- 1 medium tomato, chopped
- 2 avocados, peeled and sliced
- 1 small onion, sliced into thin rings
- Sour cream
- maize wrap crisps (optional)

1. Split each chicken breast in half lengthwise. 2. Mix lime juice, cumin, and salt together and brush on all surfaces of chicken breasts. 3. Place in air fryer basket and air fry at 200°C for 12 to 15 minutes, until well done. 4. Divide the cheese evenly over chicken breasts and cook for an additional minute to melt cheese. 5. While chicken is cooking, heat refried beans on stovetop or in microwave. 6. When ready to serve, divide beans among 4 plates. Place chicken breasts on top of beans and spoon salsa over. Arrange the lettuce, tomatoes, and avocados artfully on each plate and scatter with the onion rings. 7. Pass sour cream at the table and serve with maize wrap crisps if desired.

Spiced Merguez-Style Chicken Meatballs

Prep time: 30 minutes | Cook time: 10 minutes | Serves 4

- 450 g chicken mince
- 2 garlic cloves, finely minced
- 1 tablespoon sweet Hungarian paprika
- 1 teaspoon kosher salt
- 1 teaspoon sugar
- 1 teaspoon ground cumin
- ½ teaspoon black pepper
- ½ teaspoon ground fennel
- ½ teaspoon ground coriander
- ½ teaspoon cayenne pepper
- ¼ teaspoon ground allspice

1. In a large bowl, gently mix the chicken, garlic, paprika, salt, sugar, cumin, black pepper, fennel, coriander, cayenne, and allspice until all the ingredients are incorporated. Let stand for 30 minutes at room temperature, or cover and refrigerate for up to 24 hours. 2. Form the mixture into 16 meatballs. Arrange them in a single layer in the air fryer basket. Set the air fryer to 200°C for 10 minutes, turning the meatballs halfway through the cooking time. Use a meat thermometer to ensure the meatballs have reached an internal temperature of 76°C.

Nashville Hot Chicken

Prep time: 20 minutes | Cook time: 24 to 28 minutes | Serves 8

- 1.4 kg bone-in, skin-on chicken pieces, breasts halved crosswise
- 1 tablespoon sea salt
- 1 tablespoon freshly ground black pepper
- 70 g finely ground blanched almond flour
- 130 g grated Parmesan cheese
- 1 tablespoon baking powder
- 2 teaspoons garlic powder, divided
- 120 g heavy (whipping) cream
- 2 large eggs, beaten
- 1 tablespoon vinegar-based hot sauce
- Avocado oil spray
- 115 g unsalted butter
- 120 ml avocado oil
- 1 tablespoon cayenne pepper (more or less to taste)
- 2 tablespoons Xylitol

1. Season the chicken pieces generously with salt and pepper, ensuring even coverage on all sides. 2. In a large, shallow bowl, mix the almond flour, Parmesan cheese, baking powder, and 1 teaspoon of garlic powder until well blended. This will form the crispy breading. 3. In another bowl, whisk together the double cream, eggs, and a splash of hot sauce to create a flavorful coating. 4. Dip each chicken piece into the egg mixture, then press it into the almond flour mixture, ensuring the breading adheres firmly. Let the coated chicken rest on a plate for 15 minutes to allow the breading to set and prevent it from falling off during cooking. 5. Preheat the air fryer to 200°C. Arrange the chicken in a single layer in the air fryer basket, avoiding overcrowding. Work in batches if necessary. Spray the chicken with oil to enhance crispness, then cook for 13 minutes. 6. Carefully flip the chicken pieces using tongs, spray with more oil, and reduce the air fryer temperature to 180°C. Continue cooking for an additional 11 to 15 minutes, or until an instant-read thermometer inserted into the thickest part of the chicken reads 70°C. 7. While the chicken finishes cooking, prepare the spicy butter sauce. In a small saucepan over medium-low heat, combine the butter, avocado oil, cayenne pepper, xylitol, and the remaining teaspoon of garlic powder. Stir until the butter is melted and the sugar substitute has fully dissolved. 8. Once the chicken is cooked, remove it from the air fryer. Use tongs to dip each piece into the spicy butter sauce, ensuring a thorough coating. Place the coated chicken on a wire rack set over a baking sheet and let it rest for 5 minutes. 9. Serve the chicken warm, accompanied by your favorite dipping sauce or a crisp side salad for a satisfying meal. Enjoy the bold, spicy flavors!

Crispy Golden Chicken Tenders

Prep time: 10 minutes | Cook time: 15 minutes | Serves 4

- 60 g panko bread crumbs
- 1 tablespoon paprika
- ½ teaspoon salt
- ¼ teaspoon freshly ground black pepper
- 16 chicken tenders
- 115 g mayonnaise
- Olive oil spray

1. In a medium bowl, stir together the panko, paprika, salt, and pepper. 2. In a large bowl, toss together the chicken tenders and mayonnaise to coat. Transfer the coated chicken pieces to the bowl of seasoned panko and dredge to coat thoroughly. Press the coating onto the chicken with your fingers. 3. Insert the crisper plate into the basket and the basket into the unit. Preheat the unit by selecting AIR FRY, setting the temperature to 180°C, and setting the time to 3 minutes. Select START/STOP to begin. 4. Once the unit is preheated, place a parchment paper liner into the basket. Place the chicken into the basket and spray it with olive oil. 5. Select AIR FRY, set the temperature to 180°C, and set the time to 15 minutes. Select START/STOP to begin. 6. When the cooking is complete, the tenders will be golden brown and a food thermometer inserted into the chicken should register 76°C. For more even browning, remove the basket halfway through cooking and flip the tenders. Give them an extra spray of olive oil and reinsert the basket to resume cooking. This ensures they are crispy and brown all over. 7. When the cooking is complete, serve.

Tropical Chicken with Pineapple and Peach

Prep time: 10 minutes | Cook time: 14 to 15 minutes | Serves 4

- 1 (450 g) low-sodium boneless, skinless chicken breasts, cut into 1-inch pieces
- 1 medium red onion, chopped
- 1 (230 g) tin pineapple chunks, drained, 60 ml juice reserved
- 1 tablespoon peanut oil or safflower oil
- 1 peach, peeled, pitted, and cubed
- 1 tablespoon cornflour
- ½ teaspoon ground ginger
- ¼ teaspoon ground allspice
- Brown rice, cooked (optional)

1. Preheat the air fryer to 196°C. 2. In a medium metal bowl, mix the chicken, red onion, pineapple, and peanut oil. Bake in the air fryer for 9 minutes. Remove and stir. 3. Add the peach and return the bowl to the air fryer. Bake for 3 minutes more. Remove and stir again. 4. In a small bowl, whisk the reserved pineapple juice, the cornflour, ginger, and allspice well. Add to the chicken mixture and stir to combine. 5. Bake for 2 to 3 minutes more, or until the chicken reaches an internal temperature of 76°C on a meat thermometer and the sauce is slightly thickened. 6. Serve immediately over hot cooked brown rice, if desired.

Lemon Chicken with Garlic

Prep time: 5 minutes | Cook time: 20 to 25 minutes | Serves 4

- 8 bone-in chicken thighs, skin on
- 1 tablespoon olive oil
- 1½ teaspoons lemon-pepper seasoning
- ½ teaspoon paprika
- ½ teaspoon garlic powder
- ¼ teaspoon freshly ground black pepper
- Juice of ½ lemon

1. Begin by preheating the air fryer to 180°C to ensure even cooking. 2. In a large mixing bowl, add the chicken pieces and drizzle them generously with olive oil. Sprinkle with lemon-pepper seasoning, paprika, garlic powder, and freshly ground black pepper. Toss the chicken thoroughly, ensuring every piece is evenly coated with the flavorful seasoning mix. 3. Arrange the seasoned chicken in a single layer in the air fryer basket, leaving space between pieces for proper air circulation. Work in batches if needed to avoid overcrowding. 4. Cook the chicken in the air fryer for 20 to 25 minutes, pausing at the halfway point to flip the pieces for even browning. Use a food thermometer to ensure the thickest part of the chicken reaches an internal temperature of 76°C. 5. Once cooked, transfer the chicken to a serving platter. Finish with a generous squeeze of fresh lemon juice over the top to enhance the zesty flavor. Serve immediately and enjoy your perfectly seasoned and juicy chicken!

Crunchy Dill-Coated Chicken Strips

Prep time: 30 minutes | Cook time: 10 minutes | Serves 4

- 2 whole boneless, skinless chicken breasts (about 450 g each), halved lengthwise
- 230 ml Italian dressing
- 110 g finely crushed crisps
- 1 tablespoon dried dill
- 1 tablespoon garlic powder
- 1 large egg, beaten
- 1 to 2 tablespoons oil

1. In a large resealable bag, combine the chicken and Italian dressing. Seal the bag and refrigerate to marinate at least 1 hour. 2. In a shallow dish, stir together the potato chips, dill, and garlic powder. Place the beaten egg in a second shallow dish. 3. Remove the chicken from the marinade. Roll the chicken pieces in the egg and the crisp mixture, coating thoroughly. 4. Preheat the air fryer to 170°C. Line the air fryer basket with parchment paper. 5. Place the coated chicken on the parchment and spritz with oil. 6. Cook for 5 minutes. Flip the chicken, spritz it with oil, and cook for 5 minutes more until the outsides are crispy and the insides are no longer pink.

Zesty Pepper-Stuffed Chicken Rolls

Prep time: 10 minutes | Cook time: 12 minutes | Serves 4

- 2 (115 g) boneless, skinless chicken breasts, slice in half horizontally
- 1 tablespoon olive oil
- Juice of ½ lime
- 2 tablespoons taco seasoning
- ½ green pepper, cut into strips
- ½ red pepper, cut into strips
- ¼ onion, sliced

1. Preheat the air fryer to 200°C. 2. Unfold the chicken breast slices on a clean work surface. Rub with olive oil, then drizzle with lime juice and sprinkle with taco seasoning. 3. Top the chicken slices with equal amount of peppers and onion. Roll them up and secure with toothpicks. 4. Arrange the chicken roll-ups in the preheated air fryer. Air fry for 12 minutes or until the internal temperature of the chicken reaches at least 76°C. Flip the chicken roll-ups halfway through. 5. Remove the chicken from the air fryer. Discard the toothpicks and serve immediately.

Chicken Burgers with Gammon and Cheese

Prep time: 12 minutes | Cook time: 13 to 16 minutes | Serves 4

- 20 g soft bread crumbs
- 3 tablespoons milk
- 1 egg, beaten
- ½ teaspoon dried thyme
- Pinch salt
- Freshly ground black pepper, to taste
- 570 g chicken mince
- 70 g finely choppedgammon
- 75 g grated Gouda cheese
- Olive oil for misting

1. Begin by preheating the air fryer to 180ºC to prepare for even cooking.2. In a medium mixing bowl, combine the bread crumbs, milk, egg, thyme, salt, and pepper. Mix until well blended, then gently fold in the ground chicken, ensuring all ingredients are evenly incorporated without overmixing.3. Divide the chicken mixture into eight portions and shape each into a thin patty. Place the patties on waxed paper to prevent sticking.4. Take four of the patties and top each with a slice of gammon and a piece of cheese. Place the remaining patties on top, gently pressing the edges together to seal and encase the gammon and cheese within the burgers.5. Arrange the stuffed chicken burgers in a single layer in the air fryer basket. Lightly mist the tops with olive oil for added crispness.6. Air fry the burgers for 13 to 16 minutes, flipping halfway through. Use a meat thermometer to ensure the internal temperature of each burger reaches 76ºC for safe consumption.7. Once cooked, remove the burgers from the air fryer and serve immediately. Pair with a fresh salad, crispy fries, or your favorite dipping sauce for a complete meal. Enjoy your flavorful stuffed chicken burgers!

Zesty Chicken and Avocado Fajitas

Prep time: 10 minutes | Cook time: 10 to 14 minutes | Serves 4

- Cooking oil spray
- 4 boneless, skinless chicken breasts, sliced crosswise
- 1 small red onion, sliced
- 2 red peppers, seeded and sliced
- 120 ml spicy ranch salad dressing, divided
- ½ teaspoon dried oregano
- 8 maize wraps
- 40 g torn butter lettuce leaves
- 2 avocados, peeled, pitted, and chopped

1. Insert the crisper plate into the basket and the basket into the unit. Preheat the unit by selecting BAKE, setting the temperature to 190ºC, and setting the time to 3 minutes. Select START/STOP to begin. 2. Once the unit is preheated, spray the crisper plate with cooking oil. Place the chicken, red onion, and red pepper into the basket. Drizzle with 1 tablespoon of the salad dressing and season with the oregano. Toss to combine. 3. Select BAKE, set the temperature to 190ºC, and set the time to 14 minutes. Select START/STOP to begin. 4. After 10 minutes, check the chicken. If a food thermometer inserted into the chicken registers at least 76ºC, it is done. If not, resume cooking. 5. When the cooking is complete, transfer the chicken and vegetables to a bowl and toss with the remaining salad dressing. 6. Serve the chicken mixture family-style with the corn wraps, lettuce, and avocados, and let everyone make their own plates.

Chicken Schnitzel Hot Dogs

Prep time: 15 minutes | Cook time: 8 to 10 minutes | Serves 4

- 30 g flour
- ½ teaspoon salt
- 1 teaspoon marjoram
- 1 teaspoon dried parsley flakes
- ½ teaspoon thyme
- 1 egg
- 1 teaspoon lemon juice
- 1 teaspoon water
- 60 g bread crumbs
- 4 chicken tenders, pounded thin
- Oil for misting or cooking spray
- 4 whole-grain hotdog buns
- 4 slices Gouda cheese
- 1 small Granny Smith apple, thinly sliced
- 45 g shredded Swiss Chard cabbage
- Coleslaw dressing

1. In a shallow dish, mix flour with salt, marjoram, parsley, and thyme to create a seasoned coating base.2. In a second shallow dish, whisk together the egg, lemon juice, and water until smooth for a zesty egg wash.3. Fill a third shallow dish with bread crumbs for a crispy outer layer.4. Cut each flattened chicken tender in half lengthwise to create manageable strips.5. Dip each chicken strip first into the flour mixture, ensuring it is evenly coated. Then, dip it into the egg wash, allowing excess to drip off before rolling it thoroughly in the bread crumbs. Spray both sides of the coated chicken strips with oil or cooking spray for crisping.6. Arrange the strips in a single layer in the air fryer basket, ensuring they do not overlap. Air fry at 200ºC for 5 minutes. Flip the strips, spray the other side with oil, and continue cooking for an additional 3 to 5 minutes, or until golden brown and fully cooked through.7. To assemble, place two crispy schnitzel strips onto the bottom half of each hotdog bun. Top with slices of cheese, thinly sliced apple, and shredded cabbage for crunch and flavor.8. Drizzle generously with coleslaw dressing, then cover with the top half of the bun. Serve immediately as a unique and delicious schnitzel sandwich. Enjoy!

Chicken with Lettuce

Prep time: 15 minutes | Cook time: 14 minutes | Serves 4

- 450 g chicken breast tenders, chopped into bite-size pieces
- ½ onion, thinly sliced
- ½ red pepper, seeded and thinly sliced
- ½ green pepper, seeded and thinly sliced
- 1 tablespoon olive oil
- 1 tablespoon fajita seasoning
- 1 teaspoon kosher salt
- Juice of ½ lime
- 8 large lettuce leaves
- 230 g prepared guacamole

1. Preheat the air fryer to 200°C to ensure even cooking.2. In a large mixing bowl, combine sliced chicken, onions, and peppers. Drizzle generously with olive oil and toss until all pieces are evenly coated. Sprinkle with fajita seasoning and a pinch of salt, tossing again to ensure the seasoning is distributed evenly across the mixture.3. Arrange the chicken and vegetable mixture in a single layer in the air fryer basket, working in batches if necessary to avoid overcrowding. Cook for 14 minutes, pausing halfway to shake the basket for even cooking. Use a food thermometer to ensure the chicken reaches an internal temperature of 76°C.4. Once cooked, transfer the chicken and vegetables to a serving platter. Drizzle freshly squeezed lime juice over the top for a bright, tangy finish.5. Serve immediately with crisp lettuce leaves for wrapping and top with creamy guacamole. Enjoy your vibrant and flavorful fajita wraps for a fresh and healthy meal!

Hoisin Turkey Burgers

Prep time: 30 minutes | Cook time: 20 minutes | Serves 4

- Olive oil
- 450 g lean turkey mince
- 15 g whole-wheat bread crumbs
- 60 ml hoisin sauce
- 2 tablespoons soy sauce
- 4 whole-wheat buns

1. Lightly spray the air fryer basket with olive oil to prevent sticking and set it aside.2. In a large mixing bowl, combine ground turkey, bread crumbs, hoisin sauce, and soy sauce. Mix gently but thoroughly to create a uniform texture, avoiding overmixing to keep the patties tender.3. Divide the turkey mixture into 4 equal portions and shape each into a patty about 1 cm thick. Cover the patties with cling film and refrigerate for 30 minutes to help them firm up for cooking.4. Arrange the chilled patties in a single layer in the prepared air fryer basket, ensuring they do not touch. Lightly spray the tops with olive oil to promote browning.5. Air fry the patties at 190°C for 10 minutes. Flip them over carefully, spray the other side with olive oil, and continue cooking for an additional 5 to 10 minutes, or until the patties are golden brown and the internal temperature reaches 74°C.6. Place the cooked patties onto burger buns and top with your favorite low-calorie toppings, such as sliced tomatoes, onions, and a crunchy cabbage slaw. Serve immediately for a healthy and flavorful burger option.

Crispy Lime-Spiced Chicken Thighs

Prep time: 10 minutes | Cook time: 25 minutes | Serves 4

- 4 (115 g) bone-in, skin-on chicken thighs
- ½ teaspoon salt
- ½ teaspoon garlic powder
- 2 teaspoons chilli powder
- 1 teaspoon paprika
- 1 teaspoon ground cumin
- 1 small lime, halved

1. Pat chicken thighs dry and sprinkle with salt, garlic powder, chilli powder, paprika, and cumin. 2. Squeeze juice from ½ lime over thighs. Place thighs into ungreased air fryer basket. Adjust the temperature to 190°C and roast for 25 minutes, turning thighs halfway through cooking. Thighs will be crispy and browned with an internal temperature of at least 76°C when done. 3. Transfer thighs to a large serving plate and drizzle with remaining lime juice. Serve warm.

Crispy Herb Breaded Turkey Cutlets

Prep time: 5 minutes | Cook time: 8 minutes | Serves 4

- 30 g whole wheat bread crumbs
- ¼ teaspoon paprika
- ¼ teaspoon salt
- ¼ teaspoon black pepper
- ⅛ teaspoon dried sage
- ⅛ teaspoon garlic powder
- 1 egg
- 4 turkey breast cutlets
- Chopped fresh parsley, for serving

1. Preheat the air fryer to 192°C. 2. In a medium shallow bowl, whisk together the bread crumbs, paprika, salt, black pepper, sage, and garlic powder. 3. In a separate medium shallow bowl, whisk the egg until frothy. 4. Dip each turkey cutlet into the egg mixture, then into the bread crumb mixture, coating the outside with the crumbs. Place the breaded turkey cutlets in a single layer in the bottom of the air fryer basket, making sure that they don't touch each other. 5. Bake for 4 minutes. Turn the cutlets over, then bake for 4 minutes more, or until the internal temperature reaches 76°C. Sprinkle on the parsley and serve.

Glazed Piri-Piri Chicken Thighs

Prep time: 5 minutes | Cook time: 25 minutes | Serves 4

- 60 ml piri-piri sauce
- 1 tablespoon freshly squeezed lemon juice
- 2 tablespoons brown sugar, divided
- 2 cloves garlic, minced
- 1 tablespoon extra-virgin olive oil
- 4 bone-in, skin-on chicken thighs, each weighing approximately 200 to 230 g
- ½ teaspoon cornflour

1. To make the marinade, whisk together the piri-piri sauce, lemon juice, 1 tablespoon of brown sugar, and the garlic in a small bowl. While whisking, slowly pour in the oil in a steady stream and continue to whisk until emulsified. Using a skewer, poke holes in the chicken thighs and place them in a small glass dish. Pour the marinade over the chicken and turn the thighs to coat them with the sauce. Cover the dish and refrigerate for at least 15 minutes and up to 1 hour. 2. Preheat the air fryer to 190°C. Remove the chicken thighs from the dish, reserving the marinade, and place them skin-side down in the air fryer basket. Air fry until the internal temperature reaches 76°C, 15 to 20 minutes. 3. Meanwhile, whisk the remaining brown sugar and the cornflour into the marinade and microwave it on high power for 1 minute until it is bubbling and thickened to a glaze. 4. Once the chicken is cooked, turn the thighs over and brush them with the glaze. Air fry for a few additional minutes until the glaze browns and begins to char in spots. 5. Remove the chicken to a platter and serve with additional piri-piri sauce, if desired.

Pork Rind Fried Chicken

Prep time: 30 minutes | Cook time: 20 minutes | Serves 4

- 60 ml buffalo sauce
- 4 (115 g) boneless, skinless chicken breasts
- ½ teaspoon paprika
- ½ teaspoon garlic powder
- ¼ teaspoon ground black pepper
- 60 g g plain pork rinds, finely crushed

1. In a large resealable bowl or zip-top bag, pour the buffalo sauce over the chicken thighs. Toss the chicken thoroughly to ensure each piece is fully coated in the sauce. Seal the bowl or bag and refrigerate for at least 30 minutes, or up to overnight, to let the flavors marinate deeply.2. Remove the chicken from the marinade, allowing any excess sauce to remain on the thighs for extra flavor. Sprinkle both sides of the chicken generously with paprika, garlic powder, and black pepper for a well-seasoned crust.3. Place pork rinds into a food processor or crush them manually in a resealable bag until they form a coarse, breadcrumb-like texture. Pour the crushed pork rinds into a large shallow dish. Press each chicken thigh firmly into the pork rind crumbs, coating both sides evenly and pressing to adhere.4. Arrange the breaded chicken thighs in a single layer in the air fryer basket, leaving space between each piece for proper air circulation. Preheat the air fryer to 200°C for even cooking.5. Roast the chicken in the preheated air fryer at 200°C for 20 minutes, flipping the thighs halfway through cooking to ensure even browning. Check that the chicken reaches an internal temperature of at least 76°C for safe consumption.6. Once golden brown and crispy, remove the chicken from the air fryer. Serve immediately while hot, pairing with your favorite dipping sauce or a crisp side salad for a flavorful and satisfying meal. Enjoy!

Crispy Duck with Cherry Sauce

Prep time: 10 minutes | Cook time: 33 minutes | Serves 2 to 4

- 1 whole duck (2.3 kg), split in half, back and rib bones removed

Cherry Sauce:

- 1 tablespoon butter
- 1 shallot, minced
- 120 ml sherry
- 240 g cherry preserves
- 240 ml chicken stock
- 1 teaspoon olive oil
- Salt and freshly ground black pepper, to taste
- 1 teaspoon white wine vinegar
- 1 teaspoon fresh thyme leaves
- Salt and freshly ground black pepper, to taste

1. Preheat the air fryer to 200°C for a consistent and crispy cook.2. Trim excess fat from the duck halves, leaving a thin layer to help keep the meat moist during cooking. Rub olive oil all over the duck and generously season with salt and pepper. Place the duck halves breast side up in the air fryer basket, with the breasts facing the center for even cooking.3. Cook the duck at 200°C for 20 minutes. Flip the halves over and air fry for an additional 6 minutes to crisp up the other side.4. While the duck cooks, prepare the cherry sauce. Melt butter in a large sauté pan over medium heat. Add finely diced shallots and sauté until lightly browned, about 2 to 3 minutes. Deglaze the pan with sherry, scraping up any browned bits for added flavor. Simmer the liquid until reduced by half. Add cherry preserves, chicken stock, and white wine vinegar, whisking until smooth. Simmer the sauce until it thickens enough to coat the back of a spoon, about 5 to 7 minutes. Stir in fresh thyme leaves and season with salt and pepper to taste.5. After the initial air frying, spoon a generous layer of cherry sauce over the duck halves. Return them to the air fryer and cook for 4 more minutes at 200°C. Flip the duck halves back to breast side up, spoon more cherry sauce over the skin, and cook for an additional 3 minutes to caramelize the sauce.6. Remove the duck from the air fryer and let it rest for a few minutes to allow the juices to redistribute. Serve the duck in halves or quartered portions, spooning any remaining cherry sauce over the top or serving it on the side. Enjoy this flavorful and elegant dish!

Chicken Wings with Piri Piri Sauce

Prep time: 30 minutes | Cook time: 30 minutes | Serves 6

- 12 chicken wings
- 45 g butter, melted
- 1 teaspoon onion powder
Sauce:
- 60 g piri piri peppers, stemmed and chopped
- 1 tablespoon pimiento, seeded and minced
- 1 garlic clove, chopped
- ½ teaspoon cumin powder
- 1 teaspoon garlic paste
- 2 tablespoons fresh lemon juice
- ⅓ teaspoon sea salt
- ½ teaspoon tarragon

1. Begin by setting up a steamer basket over a saucepan of boiling water. Lower the heat to maintain a steady simmer, then place the chicken wings in the basket. Cover and steam for 10 minutes over moderate heat to partially cook and tenderize the wings.2. Remove the steamed wings and transfer them to a large bowl. Toss them thoroughly with melted butter, onion powder, cumin powder, and garlic paste, ensuring they are evenly coated with the seasoning.3. Allow the wings to cool to room temperature, then refrigerate them for 45 to 50 minutes. This step helps firm up the wings for a crispier finish during air frying.4. Preheat the air fryer to 170°C. Arrange the chilled wings in a single layer in the air fryer basket, leaving space between them for even cooking. Roast for 25 to 30 minutes, flipping halfway through, until the wings are golden brown and crispy.5. While the wings cook, prepare the Piri Piri Sauce. Combine all sauce ingredients in a food processor and blend until smooth and well mixed. Adjust the seasoning to taste if necessary.6. Once the wings are done, remove them from the air fryer and toss them in the prepared Piri Piri Sauce until fully coated. Serve immediately for a flavorful and spicy appetizer or snack. Enjoy!

Garlic Soy Chicken Thighs

Prep time: 10 minutes | Cook time: 30 minutes | Serves 1 to 2

- 2 tablespoons chicken stock
- 2 tablespoons reduced-sodium soy sauce
- 1½ tablespoons sugar
- 4 garlic cloves, smashed and peeled
- 2 large spring onions, cut into 2- to 3-inch batons, plus more, thinly sliced, for garnish
- 2 bone-in, skin-on chicken thighs (198 to 225 g each)

1. Start by preheating the air fryer to 190°C, ensuring it's ready for consistent and efficient cooking.2. In a metal cake pan, combine the chicken stock, soy sauce, and sugar, stirring until the sugar dissolves completely. Add whole garlic cloves and chopped spring onions to the mixture for aromatic depth. Submerge the chicken thighs in the marinade, turning them to coat thoroughly, and arrange them skin-side up in the pan for optimal crisping.3. Place the pan in the preheated air fryer and bake the chicken for 10 minutes. After the initial 10 minutes, begin flipping the thighs every 5 minutes, ensuring even cooking and allowing the marinade to thicken into a sticky glaze. Continue cooking for a total of about 30 minutes or until the chicken is cooked through, with the skin golden and the glaze clinging to the thighs.4. Carefully remove the pan from the air fryer and transfer the chicken thighs to a serving plate. Spoon any remaining glaze from the pan over the chicken for extra flavor, and garnish with freshly sliced spring onions for a vibrant finish.5. Serve the chicken warm, paired with steamed rice or a crisp salad, to enjoy the perfect balance of savory, sweet, and umami flavors.

Lemon Thyme Roasted Chicken

Prep time: 10 minutes | Cook time: 60 minutes | Serves 6

- 2 tablespoons baking powder
- 1 teaspoon smoked paprika
- Sea salt and freshly ground black pepper, to taste
- 900 g chicken wings or chicken drumettes
- Avocado oil spray
- 80 ml avocado oil
- 120 ml Buffalo hot sauce, such as Frank's RedHot
- 4 tablespoons unsalted butter
- 2 tablespoons apple cider vinegar
- 1 teaspoon minced garlic

1. In a large mixing bowl, combine baking powder, smoked paprika, salt, and pepper. Toss the chicken wings in the mixture until thoroughly coated for a crispy, flavorful crust.2. Preheat the air fryer to 200°C for consistent, high-heat cooking. Lightly spray the seasoned wings with oil to enhance browning and crispiness.3. Arrange the wings in a single layer in the air fryer basket, working in batches if needed to avoid overcrowding. Air fry the wings for 20 to 25 minutes, flipping halfway through. Check for doneness with an instant-read thermometer; remove the wings when they reach 70°C and let them rest until they climb to a safe 76°C.4. While the wings cook, prepare the Buffalo sauce. In a small saucepan over medium-low heat, whisk together avocado oil, hot sauce, melted butter, vinegar, and minced garlic. Heat until the mixture is warm and well combined, creating a rich, tangy sauce.5. Once the wings are done, transfer them to a large bowl and toss thoroughly with the warm Buffalo sauce, ensuring they are fully coated.6. Serve the wings immediately, garnished with fresh herbs or alongside dipping sauces like blue cheese or ranch for a classic pairing. Enjoy your crispy, flavorful wings!

Chapter 5
Fish and Seafood

Chapter 5 Fish and Seafood

Spicy Air-Fried Chilli Prawns

Prep time: 10 minutes | Cook time: 8 minutes | Serves 2

- 8 prawns, peeled and deveined
- Salt and black pepper, to taste
- ½ teaspoon ground cayenne pepper
- ½ teaspoon garlic powder
- ½ teaspoon ground cumin
- ½ teaspoon red chilli flakes
- Cooking spray

1. Preheat the air fryer to 170°C. Spritz the air fryer basket with cooking spray. 2. Toss the remaining ingredients in a large bowl until the prawns are well coated. 3. Spread the coated prawns evenly in the basket and spray them with cooking spray. 4. Air fry for 8 minutes, flipping the prawns halfway through, or until the prawns are pink. 5. Remove the prawns from the basket to a plate.

Golden Beer-Battered Cod

Prep time: 5 minutes | Cook time: 15 minutes | Serves 4

- 2 eggs
- 240 ml malty beer
- 60 g plain flour
- 30 g cornflour
- 1 teaspoon garlic powder
- Salt and pepper, to taste
- 4 cod fillets, 110 g each
- Cooking spray

1. Preheat the air fryer to 200°C to ensure even cooking and a crispy finish. 2. In a shallow bowl, whisk together the eggs and beer until frothy, creating a light batter base. In a separate shallow bowl, mix the flour and cornflour thoroughly, then season generously with garlic powder, salt, and black pepper for added flavor. 3. Coat each cod fillet by dredging it first in the flour mixture, ensuring an even layer. Next, dip the fillet into the egg and beer mixture, letting any excess drip off, and then dredge it again in the flour mixture, pressing gently to ensure a thick, even coating. 4. Spray the air fryer basket with cooking spray to prevent sticking. Arrange the coated cod fillets in a single layer in the basket, ensuring there is space between them for proper air circulation. 5. Cook the fish in the preheated air fryer for 15 minutes, flipping the fillets halfway through the cooking time. Check for doneness with a meat thermometer; the fish should reach an internal temperature of 64°C, and the outside should be golden brown and crispy. 6. Once cooked, remove the cod fillets from the air fryer and let them cool for 5 minutes to allow the coating to set. Serve immediately, paired with your favorite dipping sauce or a side of tartar sauce, along with fresh lemon wedges for a zesty finish. Enjoy your perfectly crisp air-fried fish!

Garlic Basil Prawn Pasta with Mushrooms

Prep time: 10 minutes | Cook time: 10 minutes | Serves 6

- 455 g small prawns, peeled and deveined
- 120 ml olive oil plus 1 tablespoon, divided
- ¼ teaspoon garlic powder
- ¼ teaspoon cayenne
- 455 g whole grain pasta
- 5 garlic cloves, minced
- 230 g baby mushrooms, sliced
- 45 g Parmesan, plus more for serving (optional)
- 1 teaspoon salt
- ½ teaspoon black pepper
- ½ cup fresh basil

1. Preheat the air fryer to 190°C. 2. In a small bowl, combine the prawns, 1 tablespoon olive oil, garlic powder, and cayenne. Toss to coat the prawns. 3. Place the prawns into the air fryer basket and roast for 5 minutes. Remove the prawns and set aside. 4. Cook the pasta according to package directions. Once done cooking, reserve ½ cup pasta water, then drain. 5. Meanwhile, in a large skillet, heat 120 ml of olive oil over medium heat. Add the garlic and mushrooms and cook down for 5 minutes. 6. Pour the pasta, reserved pasta water, Parmesan, salt, pepper, and basil into the skillet with the vegetable-and-oil mixture, and stir to coat the pasta. 7. Toss in the prawns and remove from heat, then let the mixture sit for 5 minutes before serving with additional Parmesan, if desired.

Crispy Bacon-Wrapped Scallops

Prep time: 5 minutes | Cook time: 10 minutes | Serves 4

- 8 sea scallops, 30 g each, cleaned and patted dry
- 8 slices bacon
- ¼ teaspoon salt
- ¼ teaspoon ground black pepper

1. Wrap each scallop in 1 slice bacon and secure with a toothpick. Sprinkle with salt and pepper. 2. Place scallops into ungreased air fryer basket. Adjust the temperature to 180°C and air fry for 10 minutes. Scallops will be opaque and firm, and have an internal temperature of 56°C when done. Serve warm.

Lemon-Tarragon Fish en Papillote

Prep time: 10 minutes | Cook time: 15 minutes | Serves 2

- 2 tablespoons salted butter, melted
- 1 tablespoon fresh lemon juice
- ½ teaspoon dried tarragon, crushed, or 2 sprigs fresh tarragon
- 1 teaspoon kosher or coarse sea salt
- 85 g julienned carrots
- 435 g julienned fennel, or 1 stalk julienned celery
- 75 g thinly sliced red pepper
- 2 cod fillets, 170 g each, thawed if frozen
- Vegetable oil spray
- ½ teaspoon black pepper

1. In a medium mixing bowl, whisk together the softened butter, fresh lemon juice, tarragon, and ½ teaspoon of salt until the mixture is smooth and creamy. Add the sliced carrots, fennel, and a dash of black pepper, tossing to coat the vegetables evenly in the sauce. Set aside.2. Cut two large squares of baking paper, each big enough to hold one fish fillet and half of the vegetable mixture. Lightly spray the fish fillets with vegetable oil spray, then season both sides with the remaining ½ teaspoon of salt and a sprinkle of black pepper for added flavor.3. Place one fish fillet on each piece of baking paper. Top each fillet with half of the prepared vegetables, ensuring an even distribution. Drizzle any remaining sauce over the vegetables for extra flavor.4. Fold the baking paper over the fish and vegetables, crimping the edges tightly in small, overlapping folds to create a sealed packet. This will trap the steam and flavors inside during cooking. Place the packets in the air fryer basket, ensuring they do not overlap.5. Air fry at 180°C for 15 minutes. The fish should be tender, flaky, and infused with the flavors of the sauce and vegetables.6. Carefully transfer the packets to serving plates. Use scissors to cut open the paper just before serving, being cautious of the hot steam inside. Serve immediately, pairing with a side of crusty bread or a light salad for a complete meal. Enjoy the aromatic and flavorful dish!

Tuna Steaks with Olive Tapenade

Prep time: 10 minutes | Cook time: 10 minutes | Serves 4

- 4 (170 g) ahi tuna steaks
- 1 tablespoon olive oil
- Salt and freshly ground black pepper, to taste
- ½ lemon, sliced into 4 wedges

Olive Tapenade:
- 90 g pitted Kalamata olives
- 1 tablespoon olive oil
- 1 tablespoon chopped fresh parsley
- 1 clove garlic
- 2 teaspoons red wine vinegar
- 1 teaspoon capers, drained

1. Preheat the air fryer to 200°C to ensure even and quick cooking.2. Brush both sides of the tuna steaks with olive oil and season generously with salt and freshly ground black pepper. Place the tuna steaks in a single layer in the air fryer basket, ensuring there is space between them for air circulation.3. Air fry the tuna steaks for 10 minutes, flipping them halfway through the cooking time. The steaks should feel firm to the touch when done but remain moist and tender on the inside.4. While the tuna cooks, prepare the tapenade. In a food processor, combine pitted olives, olive oil, fresh parsley, minced garlic, white wine vinegar, and capers. Pulse the ingredients until finely chopped, stopping to scrape down the sides of the bowl if needed. Adjust seasoning to taste, adding a pinch of salt or a squeeze of lemon if desired.5. Once the tuna steaks are cooked, transfer them to serving plates. Spoon the prepared tapenade generously over the top of each steak for a burst of flavor.6. Serve immediately, accompanied by lemon wedges for an optional zesty finish. Pair with a light side salad or roasted vegetables for a complete and satisfying meal. Enjoy!

Golden Air-Fried Crab Cakes

Prep time: 10 minutes | Cook time: 10 minutes | Serves 4

- 2 tins lump crab meat, 170 g each
- ¼ cup blanched finely ground almond flour
- 1 large egg
- 2 tablespoons full-fat mayonnaise
- ½ teaspoon Dijon mustard
- ½ tablespoon lemon juice
- ½ medium green pepper, seeded and chopped
- 235 g chopped spring onion
- ½ teaspoon Old Bay seasoning

1. In a large bowl, combine all ingredients. Form into four balls and flatten into patties. Place patties into the air fryer basket. 2. Adjust the temperature to 180°C and air fry for 10 minutes. 3. Flip patties halfway through the cooking time. Serve warm.

Crispy Parmesan-Crusted Lobster Tails

Prep time: 5 minutes | Cook time: 7 minutes | Serves 4

- 4 (110 g) lobster tails
- 2 tablespoons salted butter, melted
- 1½ teaspoons Cajun seasoning, divided
- ¼ teaspoon salt
- ¼ teaspoon ground black pepper
- 40 g grated Parmesan cheese
- 15 g pork scratchings, finely crushed

1. Cut lobster tails open carefully with a pair of scissors and gently pull meat away from shells, resting meat on top of shells. 2. Brush lobster meat with butter and sprinkle with 1 teaspoon Cajun seasoning, ¼ teaspoon per tail. 3. In a small bowl, mix remaining Cajun seasoning, salt and pepper, Parmesan, and pork scratchings. Gently press ¼ mixture onto meat on each lobster tail. 4. Carefully place tails into ungreased air fryer basket. Adjust the temperature to 200°C and air fry for 7 minutes. Lobster tails will be crispy and golden on top and have an internal temperature of at least 64°C when done. Serve warm.

Tuna Melt

Prep time: 3 minutes | Cook time: 10 minutes | Serves 1

- Olive or vegetable oil, for spraying
- 140 g canned tuna, drained
- 1 tablespoon mayonnaise
- ¼ teaspoon garlic granules, plus more for garnish
- 2 teaspoons unsalted butte
- 2 slices sandwich bread of choice
- 2 slices Cheddar cheese

1. Line the air fryer basket with baking paper and lightly coat it with cooking oil spray to prevent sticking. 2. In a medium bowl, combine the tuna, mayonnaise, and minced garlic. Mix thoroughly until the ingredients are well blended and creamy. 3. Spread 1 teaspoon of softened butter on one side of each slice of bread. Place one slice butter-side down in the prepared air fryer basket. 4. Layer the sandwich by placing a slice of cheese on the bread, followed by the tuna mixture, another slice of cheese, and then the second slice of bread, butter-side up. Press gently to ensure the sandwich holds together. 5. Air fry the sandwich at 200°C for 5 minutes. Carefully flip it over and cook for another 5 minutes, or until both sides are golden brown and crispy. 6. Remove the sandwich from the air fryer and sprinkle with a touch of additional garlic for extra flavor. Slice in half and serve immediately for a warm, cheesy, and flavorful tuna melt. Enjoy!

Creamy Fish Gratin with Swiss Cheese Topping

Prep time: 30 minutes | Cook time: 17 minutes | Serves 4

- 1 tablespoon avocado oil
- 455 g hake fillets
- 1 teaspoon garlic powder
- Sea salt and ground white pepper, to taste
- 2 tablespoons shallots, chopped
- 1 pepper, seeded and chopped
- 110 g cottage cheese
- 120 ml sour cream
- 1 egg, well whisked
- 1 teaspoon yellow mustard
- 1 tablespoon lime juice
- 60 g Swiss cheese, shredded

1. Brush the bottom and sides of a casserole dish with avocado oil. Add the hake fillets to the casserole dish and sprinkle with garlic powder, salt, and pepper. 2. Add the chopped shallots and peppers. 3. In a mixing bowl, thoroughly combine the Cottage cheese, sour cream, egg, mustard, and lime juice. Pour the mixture over fish and spread evenly. 4. Cook in the preheated air fryer at 190°C for 10 minutes. 5. Top with the Swiss cheese and cook an additional 7 minutes. Let it rest for 10 minutes before slicing and serving. Bon appétit!

Snapper with Shallot and Tomato

Prep time: 20 minutes | Cook time: 15 minutes | Serves 2

- 2 snapper fillets
- 1 shallot, peeled and sliced
- 2 garlic cloves, halved
- 1 pepper, sliced
- 1 small-sized serrano pepper, sliced
- 1 tomato, sliced
- 1 tablespoon olive oil
- ¼ teaspoon freshly ground black pepper
- ½ teaspoon paprika
- Sea salt, to taste
- 2 bay leaves

1. Lay two sheets of baking paper flat on your workspace. Position the fish in the middle of one sheet, ensuring there's enough space around the edges for folding. 2. Arrange the shallot, garlic, peppers, and tomato on top of the fish. Generously drizzle olive oil over everything, then season with a blend of black pepper, paprika, and salt. Place the bay leaves around the fish for added aroma. 3. Fold the baking paper over the fish, creating a pocket. Carefully crimp the edges all the way around, forming a tightly sealed crescent to lock in the flavors and steam. 4. Transfer the wrapped fish to a preheated air fryer set to 200°C and cook for 15 minutes until the fish is tender and infused with the seasonings. Serve immediately, unwrapping the paper at the table for a dramatic presentation!

Crispy Coconut Prawns with Spicy Lime Sauce

Prep time: 15 minutes | Cook time: 8 minutes | Serves 4

70 g pork scratchings

- 70 g desiccated, unsweetened coconut
- 45 g coconut flour
- 1 teaspoon onion powder
- 1 teaspoon garlic powder
- 2 eggs
- 680 g large prawns, peeled and deveined
- ½ teaspoon salt
- ¼ teaspoon freshly ground black pepper
- Spicy Dipping Sauce:
- 115 g mayonnaise
- 2 tablespoons Sriracha
- Zest and juice of ½ lime
- 1 clove garlic, minced

1. Preheat the air fryer to 200°C. 2. In a food processor fitted with a metal blade, combine the pork scratchings and desiccated coconut. Pulse until the mixture resembles coarse crumbs. Transfer to a shallow bowl. 3. In another shallow bowl, combine the coconut flour, onion powder, and garlic powder; mix until thoroughly combined. 4. In a third shallow bowl, whisk the eggs until slightly frothy. 5. In a large bowl, season the prawns with the salt and pepper, tossing gently to coat. 6. Working a few pieces at a time, dredge the prawns in the flour mixture, followed by the eggs, and finishing with the pork rind crumb mixture. Arrange the prawns on a baking sheet until ready to air fry. 7. Working in batches if necessary, arrange the prawns in a single layer in the air fryer basket. Pausing halfway through the cooking time to turn the prawns, air fry for 8 minutes until cooked through. 8. To make the sauce: In a small bowl, combine the mayonnaise, Sriracha, lime zest and juice, and garlic. Whisk until thoroughly combined. Serve alongside the prawns.

Roasted Salmon Fillets

Prep time: 5 minutes | Cook time: 10 minutes | Serves 2

- 2 (230 g) skin-on salmon fillets, 1½ inches thick
- 1 teaspoon vegetable oil
- Salt and pepper, to taste
- Vegetable oil spray

1. Preheat the air fryer to 200°C to prepare for even cooking. 2. Create a foil sling for the air fryer basket by folding a long sheet of aluminium foil into a 4-inch-wide strip. Lay the foil widthwise across the basket, pressing it into the bottom and up the sides. Fold any excess foil neatly so that the edges are flush with the top of the basket. Lightly spray both the foil and basket with vegetable oil spray to prevent sticking. 3. Pat the salmon fillets dry with paper towels to remove excess moisture. Rub the fillets with olive oil and season generously with salt and black pepper. Arrange the fillets skin side down on the foil sling in the prepared basket, ensuring they are spaced apart for proper airflow. 4. Air fry the salmon at 200°C for 10 to 14 minutes, rotating the sling halfway through for even cooking. Check the fillets by inserting the tip of a paring knife into the center; the salmon should be translucent in the middle and register 52°C for medium-rare. 5. Using the foil sling, carefully lift the salmon out of the air fryer. Slide a fish spatula along the underside of each fillet to separate it from the skin, leaving the skin behind on the foil. Transfer the fillets to individual serving plates. 6. Serve the salmon immediately, optionally garnished with fresh herbs or a squeeze of lemon for added flavor. Pair with your favorite sides for a complete, healthy meal. Enjoy!

Sea Bass with Crispy Potato Scales and Caper Aïoli

Prep time: 10 minutes | Cook time: 10 minutes | Serves 2

- 2 fillets of sea bass, 170- to 230 g each
- Salt and freshly ground black pepper, to taste
- 60 ml mayonnaise
- 2 teaspoons finely chopped lemon zest
- 1 teaspoon chopped fresh thyme
- 2 Fingerling, or new potatoes, very thinly sliced into rounds
- Olive oil
- ½ clove garlic, crushed into a paste
- 1 tablespoon capers, drained and rinsed
- 1 tablespoon olive oil
- 1 teaspoon lemon juice, to taste

1. Preheat the air fryer to 200°C. 2. Season the fish well with salt and freshly ground black pepper. Mix the mayonnaise, lemon zest and thyme together in a small bowl. Spread a thin layer of the mayonnaise mixture on both fillets. Start layering rows of potato slices onto the fish fillets to simulate the fish scales. The second row should overlap the first row slightly. Dabbing a little more mayonnaise along the upper edge of the row of potatoes where the next row overlaps will help the potato slices stick. Press the potatoes onto the fish to secure them well and season again with salt. Brush or spray the potato layer with olive oil. 3. Transfer the fish to the air fryer and air fry for 8 to 10 minutes, depending on the thickness of your fillets. 1-inch of fish should take 10 minutes at 200°C. 4. While the fish is cooking, add the garlic, capers, olive oil and lemon juice to the remaining mayonnaise mixture to make the caper aïoli. 5. Serve the fish warm with a dollop of the aïoli on top or on the side.

Tuna with Herbs

Prep time: 20 minutes | Cook time: 17 minutes | Serves 4

- 1 tablespoon butter, melted
- 1 medium-sized leek, thinly sliced
- 1 tablespoon chicken stock
- 1 tablespoon dry white wine
- 455 g tuna
- ½ teaspoon red pepper flakes, crushed
- Sea salt and ground black pepper, to taste
- ½ teaspoon dried rosemary
- ½ teaspoon dried basil
- ½ teaspoon dried thyme
- 2 small ripe tomatoes, puréed
- 120 g Parmesan cheese, grated

1. Begin by heating ½ tablespoon of butter in a skillet over medium heat. Sauté the leek and garlic until they soften and release a rich aroma. Pour in the stock and wine to loosen any browned bits from the pan and combine the flavors thoroughly. 2. Set the air fryer to preheat at 190°C, ensuring it's ready for cooking. 3. Coat a casserole dish evenly with the remaining melted butter. Lay the fish fillets inside, sprinkle with your preferred seasonings, and spread the leek and garlic mixture over the top. Add a layer of tomato purée to enhance the flavor. Place the dish in the preheated air fryer and cook for 10 minutes. 4. After the initial cooking, sprinkle grated Parmesan cheese generously over the fish. Return the dish to the air fryer and cook for an additional 7 minutes, or until the cheese turns golden and slightly crispy. Serve hot and enjoy your meal!

Prawns Scampi

Prep time: 8 minutes | Cook time: 8 minutes | Serves 4

- 4 tablespoons salted butter or ghee
- 1 tablespoon fresh lemon juice
- 1 tablespoon minced garlic
- 2 teaspoons red pepper flakes
- 455 g prawns (21 to 25 count), peeled and deveined
- 2 tablespoons dry white wine or chicken broth
- 2 tablespoons chopped fresh basil, plus more for sprinkling, or 1 teaspoon dried
- 1 tablespoon chopped fresh chives, or 1 teaspoon dried

1. Preheat your air fryer to 160°C with a baking pan inside for 8 minutes. This step ensures the pan is warm, allowing the butter to melt quickly and evenly. 2. Once preheated, remove the pan and add butter, lemon juice, garlic, and red pepper flakes. Return the pan to the air fryer to cook for 2 minutes, stirring once during cooking to blend the flavors. The garlic will infuse the butter, creating the foundation for the dish. 3. Carefully take the pan out again and add the prawns, broth, chopped basil, and chives. Mix everything gently to coat the prawns in the flavored butter mixture. 4. Place the pan back into the air fryer and cook for 5 minutes, stirring halfway through to ensure even cooking and coating. 5. Remove the pan and give the prawns a final stir, then let them rest for 1 minute on a wire rack. This resting time allows the prawns to finish cooking gently in the residual heat, preventing them from becoming rubbery. 6. Stir once more to ensure all flavors are evenly distributed, garnish with freshly chopped basil, and serve the dish immediately while still hot. Enjoy!

Oyster Po'Boy

Prep time: 20 minutes | Cook time: 5 minutes | Serves 4

- 55 g plain flour
- 20 g yellow cornmeal
- 1 tablespoon Cajun seasoning
- 1 teaspoon salt
- 2 large eggs, beaten
- 1 teaspoon hot sauce
- 455 g pre-shucked oysters
- 1 (12-inch) French baguette, quartered and sliced horizontally
- Tartar Sauce, as needed
- 150 g shredded lettuce, divided
- 2 tomatoes, cut into slices
- Cooking spray

1. In a shallow bowl, whisk together flour, cornmeal, Cajun seasoning, and a pinch of salt until evenly mixed. In a second shallow bowl, whisk the eggs with hot sauce to create a flavorful coating. 2. Dip each oyster into the cornmeal mixture, ensuring it's evenly coated. Then, dip it into the egg mixture, letting the excess drip off, before dredging it again in the cornmeal mixture. Press gently to adhere the coating securely. 3. Preheat the air fryer to 200°C. Line the air fryer basket with baking paper for easy cleanup and to prevent sticking. 4. Arrange the coated oysters in a single layer on the baking paper. Lightly spritz the oysters with oil to promote browning. 5. Air fry the oysters for 2 minutes. Shake the basket gently to ensure even cooking, spritz with more oil, and continue air frying for an additional 3 minutes, or until the oysters are golden brown and crispy. 6. Spread tartar sauce generously on each sandwich half. Assemble the po'boys by layering the fried oysters on the bread, followed by ½ cup of shredded lettuce and 2 slices of tomato per sandwich. 7. Serve immediately while the oysters are hot and crispy, paired with a side of fries or coleslaw for a classic po'boy experience. Enjoy!

Tex-Mex Salmon Bowl

Prep time: 15 minutes | Cook time: 9 to 14 minutes | Serves 4

- 340 g salmon fillets, cut into 1½-inch cubes
- 1 red onion, chopped
- 1 red chilli, minced
- 1 red pepper, chopped
- 60 ml salsa
- 2 teaspoons peanut or safflower oil
- 2 tablespoons tomato juice
- 1 teaspoon chilli powder

1. Begin by setting the air fryer to preheat at 190ºC, ensuring it's ready for cooking. 2. In a medium metal bowl, combine the salmon cubes, diced red onion, chopped jalapeño, red pepper, salsa, peanut oil, tomato juice, and a sprinkle of chili powder. Mix thoroughly until all ingredients are evenly coated and blended. 3. Place the metal bowl directly into the air fryer basket. Cook for 9 to 14 minutes, stirring halfway through to ensure the salmon cooks evenly and the vegetables become tender and flavorful. 4. Remove the bowl carefully from the air fryer, give the mixture a final stir, and serve immediately while warm. Enjoy the vibrant blend of flavors!

Crispy Almond-Crusted Lemon Fish

Prep time: 10 minutes | Cook time: 7 to 8 minutes | Serves 4

- 70 g raw whole almonds
- 1 spring onion, finely chopped
- Grated zest and juice of 1 lemon
- ½ tablespoon extra-virgin olive oil
- ¾ teaspoon kosher or coarse sea salt, divided
- Freshly ground black pepper, to taste
- 4 skinless fish fillets, 170 g each
- Cooking spray
- 1 teaspoon Dijon mustard

1. In a food processor, pulse the almonds to coarsely chop. Transfer to a small bowl and add the scallion, lemon zest, and olive oil. Season with ¼ teaspoon of the salt and pepper to taste and mix to combine. 2. Spray the top of the fish with oil and squeeze the lemon juice over the fish. Season with the remaining ½ teaspoon salt and pepper to taste. Spread the mustard on top of the fish. Dividing evenly, press the almond mixture onto the top of the fillets to adhere. 3. Preheat the air fryer to 190ºC. 4. Working in batches, place the fillets in the air fryer basket in a single layer. Air fry for 7 to 8 minutes, until the crumbs start to brown and the fish is cooked through. 5. Serve immediately.

Spicy Firecracker Prawns

Prep time: 10 minutes | Cook time: 7 minutes | Serves 4

- 455 g medium prawns, peeled and deveined
- 2 tablespoons salted butter, melted
- ½ teaspoon Old Bay seasoning
- ¼ teaspoon garlic powder
- 2 tablespoons Sriracha
- ¼ teaspoon powdered sweetener
- 60 ml full-fat mayonnaise
- ⅛ teaspoon ground black pepper

1. In a large bowl, toss prawns in butter, Old Bay seasoning, and garlic powder. Place prawns into the air fryer basket. 2. Adjust the temperature to 200ºC and set the timer for 7 minutes. 3. Flip the prawns halfway through the cooking time. Prawns will be bright pink when fully cooked. 4. In another large bowl, mix Sriracha, sweetener, mayonnaise, and pepper. Toss prawns in the spicy mixture and serve immediately.

Prawns with Smoky Tomato Dressing

Prep time: 5 minutes | Cook time: 8 minutes | Serves 2

- 3 tablespoons mayonnaise
- 1 tablespoon ketchup
- 1 tablespoon minced garlic
- 1 teaspoon Sriracha
- ½ teaspoon smoked paprika
- ½ teaspoon kosher or coarse sea salt
- 455 g large raw prawns (21 to 25 count), peeled (tails left on) and deveined
- Vegetable oil spray
- 50 g chopped spring onions

1. Start by mixing mayonnaise, ketchup, minced garlic, Sriracha, paprika, and a pinch of salt in a large bowl until the sauce is smooth and well combined. Add the prawns to the bowl and toss thoroughly to ensure every piece is coated evenly with the flavorful mixture. 2. Lightly coat the air fryer basket with vegetable oil spray to prevent sticking. Arrange the prawns in a single layer in the basket. Set the air fryer to 180ºC and cook for 8 minutes, tossing the prawns and giving them an additional spray of vegetable oil halfway through to enhance crispiness. 3. Once cooked, transfer the prawns to a serving dish and garnish generously with freshly chopped spring onions for a vibrant and fresh finish. Serve immediately and enjoy the bold, tangy flavors!

Sweet and Spicy Blackened Tilapia

Prep time: 15 minutes | Cook time: 8 minutes | Serves 4

- 1 large egg, beaten
- Blackened seasoning, as needed
- 2 tablespoons light brown sugar
- 4 tilapia fillets, 110g each
- Cooking spray

1. In a shallow bowl, place the beaten egg. In a second shallow bowl, stir together the Blackened seasoning and the brown sugar. 2. One at a time, dip the fish fillets in the egg, then the brown sugar mixture, coating thoroughly. 3. Preheat the air fryer to 150ºC. Line the air fryer basket with baking paper. 4. Place the coated fish on the baking paper and spritz with oil. 5. Bake for 4 minutes. Flip the fish, spritz it with oil, and bake for 4 to 6 minutes more until the fish is white inside and flakes easily with a fork. 6. Serve immediately.

Coconut Prawns with Pineapple-Lemon Sauce

Prep time: 10 minutes | Cook time: 18 minutes | Serves 4

- 60 g light brown sugar
- 2 teaspoons cornflour
- ⅛ teaspoon plus ½ teaspoon salt, divided
- 110 g crushed pineapple with syrup
- 2 tablespoons freshly squeezed lemon juice
- 1 tablespoon yellow mustard
- 680 g raw large prawns, peeled and deveined
- 2 eggs
- 30 g plain flour
- 95 g desiccated, unsweetened coconut
- ¼ teaspoon garlic granules
- Olive oil spray

1. Start by heating a medium saucepan over medium heat and combining the brown sugar, cornflour, and ⅛ teaspoon of salt. Stir constantly as the mixture heats to avoid lumps. 2. Once the sugar melts and starts forming a sauce, add the crushed pineapple with its syrup, lemon juice, and mustard. Stir continuously and let the mixture cook for 4 minutes until it thickens and reaches a boil. Let it boil for 1 minute before removing the saucepan from the heat. Set the sauce aside to cool while you prepare the prawns. 3. Arrange the prawns on a plate and use paper towels to thoroughly pat them dry, ensuring they are ready for coating. 4. Crack the eggs into a small bowl and whisk until smooth. 5. In another medium bowl, combine the flour, desiccated coconut, ½ teaspoon of salt, and garlic granules. Mix well to create an even coating mixture. 6. Preheat your air fryer to 200ºC with the crisper plate inserted into the basket. Allow it to heat completely before proceeding. 7. Dip each prawn into the whisked eggs, ensuring an even coat, and then roll it in the coconut mixture to cover it entirely. 8. Once the air fryer is preheated, place a piece of baking paper in the basket and arrange the coated prawns in a single layer. Spray them lightly with olive oil to help them crisp up. 9. Cook the prawns for 6 minutes, then remove the basket, flip the prawns over, and spray them again with olive oil. Return the basket and cook for another 3 minutes, checking for a golden-brown color. If needed, continue cooking in 1-minute increments until done. 10. Serve the crispy prawns immediately, accompanied by the cooled pineapple sauce for dipping or drizzling.

Crispy Tuna Avocado Bites

Prep time: 10 minutes | Cook time: 7 minutes | Makes 12 bites

- 280 g canned tuna, drained
- 60 ml full-fat mayonnaise
- 1 stalk celery, chopped
- 1 medium avocado, peeled, pitted, and mashed
- 25 g blanched finely ground almond flour, divided
- 2 teaspoons coconut oil

1. In a large bowl, mix tuna, mayonnaise, celery, and mashed avocado. Form the mixture into balls. 2. Roll balls in almond flour and spritz with coconut oil. Place balls into the air fryer basket. 3. Adjust the temperature to 200ºC and set the timer for 7 minutes. 4. Gently turn tuna bites after 5 minutes. Serve warm.

Prawn Bake

Prep time: 15 minutes | Cook time: 5 minutes | Serves 4

- 400 g prawns, peeled and deveined
- 1 egg, beaten
- 120 ml coconut milk
- 120 g Cheddar cheese, shredded
- ½ teaspoon coconut oil
- 1 teaspoon ground coriander

1. Combine the prawns, egg, coconut milk, grated Cheddar cheese, melted coconut oil, and ground coriander in a mixing bowl. Stir thoroughly until the mixture is evenly blended and has a creamy consistency. 2. Spoon the mixture evenly into individual baking ramekins, ensuring each is filled to about three-quarters full to allow for slight expansion during cooking. Smooth the tops for even cooking. 3. Preheat the air fryer to 200ºC, then place the ramekins into the basket. Cook for 5 minutes or until the mixture is set and lightly golden on top. Serve immediately, garnished with fresh herbs if desired.

Chilean Sea Bass with Zesty Olive Relish

Prep time: 10 minutes | Cook time: 10 minutes | Serves 2

- Olive oil spray
- 2 (170 g) Chilean sea bass fillets or other firm-fleshed white fish
- 3 tablespoons extra-virgin olive oil
- ½ teaspoon ground cumin
- ½ teaspoon kosher or coarse sea salt
- ½ teaspoon black pepper
- 60 g pitted green olives, diced
- 10 g finely diced onion
- 1 teaspoon chopped capers

1. Spray the air fryer basket with the olive oil spray. Drizzle the fillets with the olive oil and sprinkle with the cumin, salt, and pepper. Place the fish in the air fryer basket. Set the air fryer to 160°C for 10 minutes, or until the fish flakes easily with a fork. 2. Meanwhile, in a small bowl, stir together the olives, onion, and capers. 3. Serve the fish topped with the relish.

Swordfish Skewers with Mediterranean Caponata

Prep time: 15 minutes | Cook time: 20 minutes | Serves 2

- 280 g small Italian aubergine, cut into 1-inch pieces
- 170 g cherry tomatoes
- 3 spring onions, cut into 2 inches long
- 2 tablespoons extra-virgin olive oil, divided
- Salt and pepper, to taste
- 340 g skinless swordfish steaks, 1¼ inches thick, cut into 1-inch pieces
- 2 teaspoons honey, divided
- 2 teaspoons ground coriander, divided
- 1 teaspoon grated lemon zest, divided
- 1 teaspoon juice
- 4 (6-inch) wooden skewers
- 1 garlic clove, minced
- ½ teaspoon ground cumin
- 1 tablespoon chopped fresh basil

1. Preheat the air fryer to 200°C. 2. Toss aubergine, tomatoes, and spring onions with 1 tablespoon oil, ¼ teaspoon salt, and ⅛ teaspoon pepper in bowl; transfer to air fryer basket. Air fry until aubergine is softened and browned and tomatoes have begun to burst, about 14 minutes, tossing halfway through cooking. Transfer vegetables to cutting board and set aside to cool slightly. 3. Pat swordfish dry with paper towels. Combine 1 teaspoon oil, 1 teaspoon honey, 1 teaspoon coriander, ½ teaspoon lemon zest, ⅛ teaspoon salt, and pinch pepper in a clean bowl. Add swordfish and toss to coat. Thread swordfish onto skewers, leaving about ¼ inch between each piece (3 or 4 pieces per skewer). 4. Arrange skewers in air fryer basket, spaced evenly apart. (Skewers may overlap slightly.) Return basket to air fryer and air fry until swordfish is browned and registers 60°C, 6 to 8 minutes, flipping and rotating skewers halfway through cooking. 5. Meanwhile, combine remaining 2 teaspoons oil, remaining 1 teaspoon honey, remaining 1 teaspoon coriander, remaining ½ teaspoon lemon zest, lemon juice, garlic, cumin, ¼ teaspoon salt, and ⅛ teaspoon pepper in large bowl. Microwave, stirring once, until fragrant, about 30 seconds. Coarsely chop the cooked vegetables, transfer to bowl with dressing, along with any accumulated juices, and gently toss to combine. Stir in basil and season with salt and pepper to taste. Serve skewers with caponata.

Tuna Patties with Spicy Sriracha Sauce

Prep time: 10 minutes | Cook time: 10 minutes | Serves 4

- 2 (170 g) cans tuna packed in oil, drained
- 3 tablespoons almond flour
- 2 tablespoons mayonnaise

Spicy Sriracha Sauce:

- 60 g mayonnaise
- 1 tablespoon Sriracha sauce
- 1 teaspoon dried dill
- ½ teaspoon onion powder
- Pinch of salt and pepper
- 1 teaspoon garlic powder

1. Begin by setting the air fryer to 190°C and let it preheat. Cut a piece of baking paper to fit the basket and place it inside to prevent sticking. 2. Take a mixing bowl and blend together the tuna, almond flour, mayonnaise, dill, and onion powder. Add a generous pinch of salt and freshly cracked black pepper, adjusting to your taste. Mash the mixture thoroughly with a fork, ensuring a smooth and cohesive texture. 3. Scoop out portions of the tuna mixture using an ice cream scoop to ensure uniform sizes. Shape the mixture into patties, then arrange them in a single layer on the prepared baking paper. Gently press each patty down to create a flat round, approximately ½ inch thick. Cook the patties in the air fryer for 10 minutes, flipping them halfway through to achieve even browning. 4. For the Sriracha sauce, stir together mayonnaise, Sriracha, and garlic powder in a small bowl until smooth. Drizzle the sauce generously over the cooked tuna patties and serve immediately while hot.

Garlic Prawns

Prep time: 15 minutes | Cook time: 10 minutes | Serves 3

Prawns:
- Olive or vegetable oil, for spraying
- 450 g medium raw prawns, peeled and deveined
- 6 tablespoons unsalted butter, melted
- 60 g panko bread crumbs

Garlic Butter Sauce:
- 115 g unsalted butter
- 2 teaspoons garlic granules
- 2 tablespoons garlic granules
- 1 teaspoon salt
- ½ teaspoon freshly ground black pepper
- ¾ teaspoon salt (omit if using salted butter)

Make the Prawns: 1. Begin by preheating the air fryer to 200°C. Line the air fryer basket with a sheet of baking paper and lightly spray it with oil to prevent sticking. 2. In a zip-top plastic bag, combine the prawns and melted butter. Seal the bag and shake thoroughly to ensure the prawns are completely coated in the butter. 3. Prepare a breading mixture by combining breadcrumbs, minced garlic, salt, and black pepper in a medium bowl. Mix well to evenly distribute the flavors. 4. Transfer the butter-coated prawns into the breadcrumb mixture. Toss gently until all the prawns are fully coated. Shake off any excess crumbs to avoid clumping during cooking. 5. Arrange the breaded prawns in a single layer in the prepared air fryer basket and give them a light spray of oil for added crispiness. 6. Cook in the air fryer for 8 to 10 minutes, flipping the prawns halfway through cooking (at around 4 to 5 minutes) and spraying lightly with oil again. Cook until the prawns are golden brown and crispy.
Make the Garlic Butter Sauce: 7. In a microwave-safe bowl, combine the butter, minced garlic, and a pinch of salt. Microwave on 50% power in 15-second intervals, stirring each time, until the butter is fully melted and infused with garlic flavor (this should take about 30 to 60 seconds). 8. Serve the crispy prawns immediately, paired with the warm garlic butter sauce on the side for dipping. Enjoy the deliciously rich and flavorful dish!

Crispy Tuna Patties with Beer Cheese Sauce

Prep time: 5 minutes | Cook time: 17 to 18 minutes | Serves 4

Tuna Patties:
- 455 g canned tuna, drained
- 1 egg, whisked
- 2 tablespoons shallots, minced
- 1 garlic clove, minced

Cheese Sauce:
- 1 tablespoon butter
- 240 ml beer
- 1 cup grated Romano cheese
- Sea salt and ground black pepper, to taste
- 1 tablespoon sesame oil
- 2 tablespoons grated Cheddar cheese

1. Mix together the canned tuna, whisked egg, shallots, garlic, cheese, salt, and pepper in a large bowl and stir to incorporate. 2. Divide the tuna mixture into four equal portions and form each portion into a patty with your hands. Refrigerate the patties for 2 hours. 3. When ready, brush both sides of each patty with sesame oil. 4. Preheat the air fryer to 180°C. 5. Place the patties in the air fryer basket and bake for 14 minutes, flipping the patties halfway through, or until lightly browned and cooked through. 6. Meanwhile, melt the butter in a pan over medium heat. 7. Pour in the beer and whisk constantly, or until it begins to bubble. 8. Add the grated Colby cheese and mix well. Continue cooking for 3 to 4 minutes, or until the cheese melts. Remove the patties from the basket to a plate. Drizzle them with the cheese sauce and serve immediately.

Chapter 6

Beef, Pork, and Lamb

Chapter 6 Beef, Pork, and Lamb

Savory Beef and Pork Banger Meatloaf

Prep time: 20 minutes | Cook time: 25 minutes | Serves 4

- 340 g beef mince
- 110 g pork banger meat
- 235 g shallots, finely chopped
- 2 eggs, well beaten
- 3 tablespoons milk
- 1 tablespoon oyster sauce
- 1 teaspoon porcini mushrooms
- ½ teaspoon cumin powder
- 1 teaspoon garlic paste
- 1 tablespoon fresh parsley
- Salt and crushed red pepper flakes, to taste
- 235 g crushed cream crackers
- Cooking spray

1. Preheat the air fryer to 180ºC. Spritz a baking dish with cooking spray. 2. Mix all the ingredients in a large bowl, combining everything well. 3. Transfer to the baking dish and bake in the air fryer for 25 minutes. 4. Serve hot.

Blackened Steak Nuggets

Prep time: 10 minutes | Cook time: 7 minutes | Serves 2

- 450 g rib eye steak, cut into 1-inch cubes
- 2 tablespoons salted melted butter
- ½ teaspoon paprika
- ½ teaspoon salt
- ¼ teaspoon garlic powder
- ¼ teaspoon onion granules
- ¼ teaspoon ground black pepper
- ⅛ teaspoon cayenne pepper

1. Begin by placing the steak pieces into a large mixing bowl. Pour melted butter over the steak and toss thoroughly to ensure every piece is coated. Add the remaining ingredients, sprinkling them evenly, and mix well to cover all sides of the steak bites with seasoning. 2. Transfer the seasoned steak bites into the air fryer basket, spreading them out in a single layer without overlapping. Set the air fryer temperature to 200ºC and cook for 7 minutes, shaking the basket three times during the process to promote even cooking. The steak bites should be crispy on the outside and browned. Ensure the internal temperature reaches at least 64ºC for medium or 82ºC for well-done. Serve immediately while warm for the best taste and texture.

Bacon-Wrapped Meat Roll

Prep time: 5 minutes | Cook time: 1 hour | Serves 4

- 30 slices thick-cut bacon
- 110 g Cheddar cheese, shredded
- 340 g steak
- 280 g pork banger meat
- Salt and ground black pepper, to taste

1. Preheat the air fryer to 200ºC. 2. Lay out 30 slices of bacon in a woven pattern and bake for 20 minutes until crisp. Put the cheese in the center of the bacon. 3. Combine the steak and banger to form a meaty mixture. 4. Lay out the meat in a rectangle of similar size to the bacon strips. Season with salt and pepper. 5. Roll the meat into a tight roll and refrigerate. 6. Preheat the air fryer to 200ºC. 7. Make a 7×7 bacon weave and roll the bacon weave over the meat, diagonally. 8. Bake for 60 minutes or until the internal temperature reaches at least 74ºC. 9. Let rest for 5 minutes before serving.

Garlic Rosemary Ribeye Steaks

Prep time: 10 minutes | Cook time: 15 minutes | Serves 2

- 60 g butter
- 1 clove garlic, minced
- Salt and ground black pepper, to taste
- 1½ tablespoons balsamic vinegar
- 60 g rosemary, chopped
- 2 ribeye steaks

1. Melt the butter in a frying pan over medium heat. Add the garlic and fry until fragrant. 2. Remove the frying pan from the heat and add the salt, pepper, and vinegar. Allow it to cool. 3. Add the rosemary, then pour the mixture into a Ziploc bag. 4. Put the ribeye steaks in the bag and shake well, coating the meat well. Refrigerate for an hour, then allow to sit for a further twenty minutes. 5. Preheat the air fryer to 200ºC. 6. Air fry the ribeye steaks for 15 minutes. 7. Take care when removing the steaks from the air fryer and plate up. 8. Serve immediately.

Bacon-Wrapped Pork Tenderloin

Prep time: 30 minutes | Cook time: 22 to 25 minutes | Serves 6

- 120 g minced onion
- 120 ml apple cider, or apple juice
- 60 ml honey
- 1 tablespoon minced garlic
- ¼ teaspoon salt
- ¼ teaspoon freshly ground black pepper
- 900 g pork tenderloin
- 1 to 2 tablespoons oil
- 8 uncooked bacon slices

1. In a medium bowl, mix together the onion, cider, honey, minced garlic, salt, and pepper until well combined. Pour the mixture into a large resealable bag or airtight container, add the pork, and seal tightly. Place in the refrigerator and marinate for at least 2 hours to infuse the flavors. 2. Preheat the air fryer to 200°C and line the basket with parchment paper to prevent sticking and simplify cleanup. 3. Remove the pork from the marinade, letting any excess liquid drip off. Place the pork onto the prepared parchment and lightly spritz it with oil for added crispness. 4. Cook the pork in the air fryer for 15 minutes, ensuring the surface starts to brown and lock in the flavors. 5. Wrap the pork with slices of bacon, securing them with toothpicks for a snug fit. Flip the pork roast, spritz it with oil again, and cook for an additional 7 to 10 minutes, or until the internal temperature reaches 64°C. Allow the pork to rest for 5 minutes after removing it from the fryer to finish cooking and retain its juices. Slice and serve for a deliciously tender dish.

Macadamia-Crusted Pork Rack

Prep time: 5 minutes | Cook time: 35 minutes | Serves 2

- 1 clove garlic, minced
- 2 tablespoons olive oil
- 450 g rack of pork
- 235 g chopped macadamia nuts
- 1 tablespoon breadcrumbs
- 1 tablespoon rosemary, chopped
- 1 egg
- Salt and ground black pepper, to taste

1. Preheat the air fryer to 180°C. 2. Combine the garlic and olive oil in a small bowl. Stir to mix well. 3. On a clean work surface, rub the pork rack with the garlic oil and sprinkle with salt and black pepper on both sides. 4. Combine the macadamia nuts, breadcrumbs, and rosemary in a shallow dish. Whisk the egg in a large bowl. 5. Dredge the pork in the egg, then roll the pork over the macadamia nut mixture to coat well. Shake the excess off. 6. Arrange the pork in the preheated air fryer and air fry for 30 minutes on both sides. Increase to 200°C and fry for 5 more minutes or until the pork is well browned. 7. Serve immediately.

Cajun Bacon-Wrapped Pork Loin Fillet

Prep time: 30 minutes | Cook time: 20 minutes | Serves 6

- 680 g pork loin fillet or pork tenderloin
- 3 tablespoons olive oil
- 2 tablespoons Cajun spice mix
- Salt, to taste
- 6 slices bacon
- Olive oil spray

1. Cut the pork in half so that it will fit in the air fryer basket. 2. Place both pieces of meat in a resealable plastic bag. Add the oil, Cajun seasoning, and salt to taste, if using. Seal the bag and massage to coat all of the meat with the oil and seasonings. Marinate in the refrigerator for at least 1 hour or up to 24 hours. 3. Remove the pork from the bag and wrap 3 bacon slices around each piece. Spray the air fryer basket with olive oil spray. Place the meat in the air fryer. Set the air fryer to 180°C for 15 minutes. Increase the temperature to 200°C for 5 minutes. Use a meat thermometer to ensure the meat has reached an internal temperature of 64°C. 4. Let the meat rest for 10 minutes. Slice into 6 medallions and serve.

Mushroom in Bacon-Wrapped Filets Mignons

Prep time: 10 minutes | Cook time: 13 minutes per batch | Serves 8

- 30 g dried porcini mushrooms
- ½ teaspoon granulated white sugar
- ½ teaspoon salt
- ½ teaspoon ground white pepper
- 8 (110 g) filets mignons or beef fillet steaks
- 8 thin-cut bacon strips

1. Start by preheating the air fryer to 200°C to ensure even cooking. 2. Place the mushrooms, sugar, salt, and white pepper into a spice grinder and blend until the mixture becomes a fine, even seasoning. 3. Lay the filet mignons on a clean surface and generously rub them with the prepared mushroom seasoning. Wrap each filet tightly with a strip of bacon, securing it with toothpicks if needed to hold the bacon in place. 4. Carefully position the bacon-wrapped filets in the air fryer basket with the seam side facing down. To ensure proper air circulation, cook in batches if necessary, leaving space between each piece. 5. Cook the filets at 200°C for 13 minutes, flipping them halfway through for even browning. For medium rare, check that the internal temperature aligns with your preference. 6. Remove the filets from the air fryer and serve them immediately while they are hot and juicy, allowing the flavors to shine.

Beef Burger

Prep time: 20 minutes | Cook time: 12 minutes | Serves 4

- 570 g lean beef mince
- 1 tablespoon soy sauce or tamari
- 1 teaspoon Dijon mustard
- ½ teaspoon smoked paprika
- 1 teaspoon shallot powder
- 1 clove garlic, minced
- ½ teaspoon cumin powder
- 60 g spring onions, minced
- ⅓ teaspoon sea salt flakes
- ⅓ teaspoon freshly cracked mixed peppercorns
- 1 teaspoon celery salt
- 1 teaspoon dried parsley

1. Combine all the listed ingredients in a mixing bowl and knead thoroughly until the mixture is fully blended and smooth. 2. Divide the mixture into four equal portions and shape each one into a round patty. Press a shallow indentation into the center of each patty to help them cook evenly and avoid puffing up during air frying. 3. Lightly spritz all sides of the patties with nonstick cooking spray to promote a golden, crisp exterior. Place the patties in the air fryer basket, ensuring they are evenly spaced, and cook at 180°C for about 12 minutes. 4. Use an instant-read thermometer to check for doneness; the internal temperature should reach 72°C to ensure safe cooking. Once ready, serve immediately and enjoy!

Italian Pork Loin

Prep time: 30 minutes | Cook time: 16 minutes | Serves 3

- 1 teaspoon sea salt
- ½ teaspoon black pepper, freshly cracked
- 60 ml red wine
- 2 tablespoons mustard
- 2 garlic cloves, minced
- 450 g pork loin joint
- 1 tablespoon Italian herb seasoning blend

1. In a ceramic bowl, combine salt, black pepper, red wine, mustard, and minced garlic to create a flavorful marinade. Submerge the pork loin in the mixture, ensuring it is fully coated, and let it marinate for at least 30 minutes to absorb the flavors. 2. Prepare the air fryer by spritzing the sides and bottom of the basket with nonstick cooking spray to prevent sticking and enhance browning. 3. Place the marinated pork loin into the air fryer basket and generously sprinkle it with an Italian herb seasoning blend for added aroma. Cook at 190°C for 10 minutes, flipping the pork halfway through. Spritz it with cooking oil during the flip to promote even crisping. 4. Continue cooking for an additional 5 to 6 minutes, or until the pork loin reaches an internal temperature of 63°C for juicy results. Remove from the air fryer and serve immediately to enjoy its full flavor and tenderness.

Tuscan Herb-Crusted Veal Loin

Prep time: 1 hour 10 minutes | Cook time: 12 minutes | Makes 3 veal chops

- 1½ teaspoons crushed fennel seeds
- 1 tablespoon minced fresh rosemary leaves
- 1 tablespoon minced garlic
- 1½ teaspoons lemon zest
- 1½ teaspoons salt
- ½ teaspoon red pepper flakes
- 2 tablespoons olive oil
- 3 (280 g) bone-in veal loin, about ½ inch thick

1. Combine all the ingredients, except for the veal loin, in a large bowl. Stir to mix well. 2. Dunk the loin in the mixture and press to submerge. Wrap the bowl in plastic and refrigerate for at least an hour to marinate. 3. Preheat the air fryer to 200°C. 4. Arrange the veal loin in the preheated air fryer and air fry for 12 minutes for medium-rare, or until it reaches your desired doneness. 5. Serve immediately.

Kheema Meatloaf

Prep time: 10 minutes | Cook time: 15 minutes | Serves 4

- 450 g 85% lean beef mince
- 2 large eggs, lightly beaten
- 235 g diced brown onion
- 60 g chopped fresh coriander
- 1 tablespoon minced fresh ginger
- 1 tablespoon minced garlic
- 2 teaspoons garam masala
- 1 teaspoon coarse or flaky salt
- 1 teaspoon ground turmeric
- 1 teaspoon cayenne pepper
- ½ teaspoon ground cinnamon
- ⅛ teaspoon ground cardamom

1. In a large mixing bowl, combine the beef mince, eggs, finely chopped onion, fresh coriander, grated ginger, minced garlic, garam masala, salt, turmeric, cayenne pepper, ground cinnamon, and cardamom. Mix gently but thoroughly to ensure all ingredients are evenly distributed without overworking the meat. 2. Transfer the seasoned meat mixture into a baking tray, shaping it evenly to ensure consistent cooking. Place the tray into the air fryer basket. Set the air fryer to 180°C and cook for 15 minutes. Use a meat thermometer to check the internal temperature, ensuring it reaches 72°C for medium doneness. 3. Carefully remove the baking tray from the air fryer and drain off any excess fat or liquid. Let the meatloaf rest for 5 minutes to allow the juices to redistribute and make slicing easier. 4. Slice the meatloaf into even portions and serve hot. Enjoy the flavorful blend of spices in every bite!

Banger and Peppers

Prep time: 7 minutes | Cook time: 35 minutes | Serves 4

- Oil, for spraying
- 900 g hot or sweet Italian-seasoned banger links, cut into thick slices
- 4 large peppers of any color, seeded and cut into slices
- 1 onion, thinly sliced
- 1 tablespoon olive oil
- 1 tablespoon chopped fresh parsley
- 1 teaspoon dried oregano
- 1 teaspoon dried basil
- 1 teaspoon balsamic vinegar

1. Prepare the air fryer basket by lining it with parchment paper and lightly spraying it with oil to prevent sticking.2. Place the banger pieces, sliced peppers, and chopped onion into a large mixing bowl, ensuring they are well combined for even cooking.3. In a separate small bowl, whisk together olive oil, fresh parsley, oregano, basil, and balsamic vinegar until emulsified. Pour this flavorful mixture over the banger, peppers, and onion, then toss thoroughly to ensure every ingredient is coated evenly.4. Use a slotted spoon to transfer the coated mixture into the prepared air fryer basket, allowing excess liquid to drain before placing it in to avoid sogginess.5. Set the air fryer to 180ºC and cook the mixture for 20 minutes. Stir well to redistribute, then continue cooking for an additional 15 minutes or until the banger is fully browned and the juices run clear. Serve immediately while hot for maximum flavor.

Air Fried Beef Satay with Peanut Dipping Sauce

Prep time: 30 minutes | Cook time: 5 to 7 minutes | Serves 4

- 230 g bavette or skirt steak, sliced into 8 strips
- 2 teaspoons curry powder
- ½ teaspoon coarse or flaky salt
- Cooking spray
- Peanut Dipping sauce:
- 2 tablespoons creamy peanut butter
- 1 tablespoon reduced-salt soy sauce
- 2 teaspoons rice vinegar
- 1 teaspoon honey
- 1 teaspoon grated ginger
- Special Equipment:
- 4 bamboo skewers, cut into halves and soaked in water for 20 minutes to keep them from burning while cooking

1. Begin by preheating the air fryer to 180ºC and lightly coating the basket with cooking spray to prevent sticking.2. In a mixing bowl, toss the steak strips with curry powder and a pinch of coarse or flaky salt, ensuring they are evenly seasoned. Thread the seasoned strips onto pre-soaked skewers, pressing gently to secure them.3. Place the prepared skewers in the air fryer basket, ensuring they are spaced apart for even cooking. Lightly spritz the skewers with cooking spray for added crispness. Cook at 180ºC for 5 to 7 minutes, turning them halfway through, until the beef is browned and cooked through.4. While the beef cooks, prepare the dipping sauce by combining peanut butter, soy sauce, rice vinegar, honey, and grated ginger in a bowl. Stir well until the mixture is smooth and creamy.5. Once the beef is done, transfer the skewers to serving plates and let them rest for 5 minutes to retain their juices. Serve alongside the peanut dipping sauce for a flavorful finish.

Swedish Meatloaf

Prep time: 10 minutes | Cook time: 35 minutes | Serves 8

- 680 g beef mince (85% lean)
- 110 g pork mince
- 1 large egg (omit for egg-free)
- 120 g minced onions
- 60 ml tomato sauce

Sauce:

- 120 g (1 stick) unsalted butter
- 120 g shredded Swiss or mild Cheddar cheese (about 60 g)
- 60 g cream cheese (60 ml),
- 2 tablespoons mustard powder
- 2 cloves garlic, minced
- 2 teaspoons fine sea salt
- 1 teaspoon ground black pepper, plus more for garnish

softened
- 80 ml beef stock
- ⅛ teaspoon ground nutmeg
- Halved cherry tomatoes, for serving (optional)

1. Preheat the air fryer to 200ºC to prepare for cooking.2. In a large mixing bowl, combine the beef, pork, egg, onions, tomato sauce, mustard powder, garlic, salt, and pepper. Use your hands to mix thoroughly until the ingredients are well blended into a uniform mixture.3. Transfer the meatloaf mixture into a loaf pan and smooth the top. Place the pan in the air fryer basket and cook for 35 minutes, or until the internal temperature reaches 64ºC. Check after 25 minutes; if the top is browning too quickly, loosely cover with foil to prevent overcooking.4. While the meatloaf bakes, prepare the sauce. Heat butter in a saucepan over medium-high heat, stirring constantly until it sizzles and brown flecks form. Reduce the heat to low and whisk in Swiss cheese, cream cheese, stock, and nutmeg. Simmer gently for at least 10 minutes, stirring occasionally, to develop deep flavors.5. Once the meatloaf is fully cooked, carefully transfer it to a serving platter. Pour the warm sauce over the top, then garnish with ground black pepper and cherry tomatoes, if desired. Let the meatloaf rest for 10 minutes to prevent crumbling before slicing.6. Store any leftovers in an airtight container, keeping them in the refrigerator for up to 3 days or in the freezer for up to 1 month. To reheat, use a preheated air fryer at 180ºC for about 4 minutes or until thoroughly warmed.

Crispy Air-Fried Chicken-Fried Steak with Gravy

Prep time: 20 minutes | Cook time: 14 minutes | Serves 2

Steak:
- Oil, for spraying
- 90 g plain flour
- 1 teaspoon salt
- 1 teaspoon freshly ground black pepper
- ½ teaspoon paprika
- ½ teaspoon onion granules
- 1 teaspoon granulated garlic
- 180 g buttermilk
- ½ teaspoon hot sauce
- 2 (140 g) minute steaks

Gravy:
- 2 tablespoons unsalted butter
- 2 tablespoons plain flour
- 235 ml milk
- ½ teaspoon salt
- ½ teaspoon freshly ground black pepper

Make the Steak 1. Line the air fryer basket with parchment and spray lightly with oil. 2. In a medium bowl, mix together the flour, salt, black pepper, paprika, onion granules, and garlic. 3. In another bowl, whisk together the buttermilk and hot sauce. 4. Dredge the steaks in the flour mixture, dip in the buttermilk mixture, and dredge again in the flour until completely coated. Shake off any excess flour. 5. Place the steaks in the prepared basket and spray liberally with oil. 6. Air fry at 200ºC for 7 minutes, flip, spray with oil, and cook for another 6 to 7 minutes, or until crispy and browned. Make the Gravy 7. In a small saucepan, whisk together the butter and flour over medium heat until the butter is melted. Slowly add the milk, salt, and black pepper, increase the heat to medium-high, and continue to cook, stirring constantly, until the mixture thickens. Remove from the heat. 8. Transfer the steaks to plates and pour the gravy over the top. Serve immediately.

Spiced Air-Fried Pork Loin Ribs with Barbecue Glaze

Prep time: 5 minutes | Cook time: 25 minutes | Serves 4

- 900 g pork loin Back Ribs
- 2 teaspoons chilli powder
- 1 teaspoon paprika
- ½ teaspoon onion granules
- ½ teaspoon garlic powder
- ¼ teaspoon ground cayenne pepper
- 120 ml low-carb, sugar-free barbecue sauce

1. Rub ribs with all ingredients except barbecue sauce. Place into the air fryer basket. 2. Adjust the temperature to 200ºC and roast for 25 minutes. 3. When done, ribs will be dark and charred with an internal temperature of at least 85ºC. Brush ribs with barbecue sauce and serve warm.

Cheesy Crescent Dogs

Prep time: 15 minutes | Cook time: 8 minutes | Makes 24 crescent dogs

- Oil, for spraying
- 1 (230 g) tin ready-to-bake croissants
- 8 slices Cheddar cheese, cut into thirds
- 1 tablespoon sea salt flakes
- 24 cocktail bangers or 8 (6-inch) hot dogs, cut into thirds
- 2 tablespoons unsalted melted butter

1. Line the air fryer basket with parchment and spray lightly with oil. 2. Separate the dough into 8 triangles. Cut each triangle into 3 narrow triangles so you have 24 total triangles. 3. Top each triangle with 1 piece of cheese and 1 cocktail banger. 4. Roll up each piece of dough, starting at the wide end and rolling toward the point. 5. Place the rolls in the prepared basket in a single layer. You may need to cook in batches, depending on the size of your air fryer. 6. Air fry at 160ºC for 3 to 4 minutes, flip, and cook for another 3 to 4 minutes, or until golden brown. 7. Brush with the melted butter and sprinkle with the sea salt flakes before serving.

Peppercorn-Crusted Beef Fillet

Prep time: 10 minutes | Cook time: 25 minutes | Serves 6

- 2 tablespoons salted melted butter
- 2 teaspoons minced roasted garlic
- 3 tablespoons ground 4-peppercorn blend
- 1 (900 g) beef fillet, trimmed of visible fat

1. In a small bowl, combine softened butter with roasted garlic, mixing until smooth. Generously brush the mixture over the entire surface of the beef fillet to enhance flavor and moisture. 2. Spread the ground peppercorns evenly across a flat plate. Roll the buttered fillet through the peppercorns, pressing gently to create a flavorful crust that coats all sides. Place the prepared fillet into the air fryer basket. 3. Set the air fryer to 200ºC and cook the beef fillet for 25 minutes. This high temperature ensures a beautifully roasted exterior. 4. At the halfway point, carefully turn the fillet to promote even cooking and maintain a consistent crust. 5. Once cooked, remove the fillet from the air fryer and let it rest for 10 minutes to allow the juices to redistribute. Slice and serve immediately for the best texture and flavor.

Thyme & Parsley Buttered Beef Fillet

Prep time: 5 minutes | Cook time: 15 minutes | Serves 4

- 1 tablespoon melted butter
- ¼ dried thyme
- 1 teaspoon garlic salt
- ¼ teaspoon dried parsley
- 450 g beef fillet

1. Preheat the air fryer to 200°C. 2. In a bowl, combine the melted butter, thyme, garlic salt, and parsley. 3. Cut the beef fillet into slices and generously apply the seasoned butter using a brush. Transfer to the air fryer basket. 4. Air fry the beef for 15 minutes. 5. Take care when removing it and serve hot.

Lamb Chops with Horseradish Sauce

Prep time: 30 minutes | Cook time: 13 minutes | Serves 4

Lamb:
- 4 lamb loin chops
- 2 tablespoons vegetable oil
- 1 clove garlic, minced
- ½ teaspoon coarse or flaky salt
- ½ teaspoon black pepper

Horseradish Cream Sauce:
- 120 ml mayonnaise
- 1 tablespoon Dijon mustard
- 1 to 1½ tablespoons grated horseradish
- 2 teaspoons sugar
- Vegetable oil spray

1. Prepare the lamb chops by brushing them generously with oil, rubbing them with minced garlic, and seasoning thoroughly with salt and pepper. Let them marinate at room temperature for 30 minutes to enhance flavor.2. While the lamb marinates, make the horseradish sauce by combining mayonnaise, mustard, horseradish, and sugar in a medium bowl. Mix until smooth and well blended. Reserve half of the sauce in a separate dish for serving.3. Lightly spray the air fryer basket with vegetable oil to prevent sticking. Arrange the lamb chops in the basket, ensuring they do not overlap. Cook at 160°C for 10 minutes, flipping the chops halfway through for even cooking.4. Remove the lamb chops from the air fryer and place them in the bowl with the horseradish sauce. Toss gently to coat them thoroughly. Return the coated chops to the air fryer basket and increase the temperature to 200°C. Cook for an additional 3 minutes, or until a meat thermometer reads an internal temperature of 64°C for medium-rare.5. Transfer the lamb chops to a serving platter and serve hot with the reserved horseradish sauce on the side for dipping. Enjoy the flavorful combination of tender lamb and zesty sauce.

Greek-Style Herb-Infused Meatloaf

Prep time: 5 minutes | Cook time: 25 minutes | Serves 6

- 450 g lean beef mince
- 2 eggs
- 2 plum tomatoes, diced
- ½ brown onion, diced
- 60 g whole wheat bread crumbs
- 1 teaspoon garlic powder
- 1 teaspoon dried oregano
- 1 teaspoon dried thyme
- 1 teaspoon salt
- 1 teaspoon black pepper
- 60 g mozzarella cheese, shredded
- 1 tablespoon olive oil
- Fresh chopped parsley, for garnish

1. Preheat the oven to 190°C. 2. In a large bowl, mix together the beef, eggs, tomatoes, onion, bread crumbs, garlic powder, oregano, thyme, salt, pepper, and cheese. 3. Form into a loaf, flattening to 1-inch thick. 4. Brush the top with olive oil, then place the meatloaf into the air fryer basket and cook for 25 minutes. 5. Remove from the air fryer and allow to rest for 5 minutes, before slicing and serving with a sprinkle of parsley.

Bacon and Cheese Stuffed Pork Chops

Prep time: 10 minutes | Cook time: 12 minutes | Serves 4

- 15 g plain pork scratchings, finely crushed
- 120 g shredded sharp Cheddar cheese
- 4 slices cooked bacon, crumbled
- 4 (110 g) boneless pork chops
- ½ teaspoon salt
- ¼ teaspoon ground black pepper

1. In a small mixing bowl, combine crushed pork scratchings, shredded Cheddar cheese, and crumbled bacon, stirring until evenly mixed to create a flavorful stuffing.2. Using a sharp knife, cut a 3-inch pocket into the side of each pork chop. Carefully stuff each pocket with about ¼ of the pork rind mixture, pressing gently to secure the filling. Season both sides of the pork chops with salt and pepper for extra flavor.3. Arrange the stuffed pork chops in the air fryer basket with the stuffed side facing up. There's no need to grease the basket. Set the air fryer to 200°C and cook for 12 minutes, allowing the chops to become golden and crisp.4. Check the pork chops for doneness using a meat thermometer; the internal temperature should be at least 64°C for safe consumption. Remove from the air fryer and serve immediately while warm, enjoying the melted cheesy stuffing with every bite.

Tomato and Bacon Zoodles

Prep time: 10 minutes | Cook time: 15 to 22 minutes | Serves 2

- 230 g sliced bacon
- 120 g baby plum tomatoes
- 1 large courgette, spiralized
- 120 g ricotta cheese
- 60 ml double/whipping cream
- 80 g finely grated Parmesan cheese, plus more for serving
- Sea salt and freshly ground black pepper, to taste

1. Preheat the air fryer to 200°C. Lay the bacon strips in a single layer in the basket, allowing slight overlap since the bacon will shrink during cooking. Work in batches if necessary to avoid overcrowding. Cook for 8 minutes, then flip the strips and air fry for an additional 2 to 5 minutes until crisp. Remove the bacon and set aside to cool. 2. Place the tomatoes into the air fryer basket and cook at 200°C for 3 to 5 minutes, until they begin to burst and release their juices. Remove the tomatoes and set them aside. 3. Add the courgette noodles to the air fryer and cook at 200°C for 2 to 4 minutes, depending on your preferred level of tenderness. Remove the noodles once they are done. 4. While the courgette cooks, prepare the sauce. In a saucepan over medium-low heat, combine the ricotta, cream, and Parmesan cheese. Stir continuously until the mixture is smooth, warm, and well blended. 5. Crumble the bacon into bite-sized pieces. In a large bowl, combine the cooked courgette noodles, crumbled bacon, and burst tomatoes. Pour the ricotta sauce over the top and toss gently to coat evenly. Season with salt and pepper to taste, then sprinkle with additional Parmesan cheese for extra flavor. Serve immediately.

Air-Fried Sirloin with Honey-Mustard Butter

Prep time: 5 minutes | Cook time: 14 minutes | Serves 4

- 900 g beef sirloin steak
- 1 teaspoon cayenne pepper
- 1 tablespoon honey
- 1 tablespoon Dijon mustard
- ½ stick butter, softened
- Sea salt and freshly ground black pepper, to taste
- Cooking spray

1. Preheat the air fryer to 200°C and spritz with cooking spray. 2. Sprinkle the steak with cayenne pepper, salt, and black pepper on a clean work surface. 3. Arrange the steak in the preheated air fryer and spritz with cooking spray. 4. Air fry for 14 minutes or until browned and reach your desired doneness. Flip the steak halfway through. 5. Meanwhile, combine the honey, mustard, and butter in a small bowl. Stir to mix well. 6. Transfer the air fried steak onto a plate and baste with the honey-mustard butter before serving.

Vietnamese Shaking Beef with Fresh Herb Salad

Prep time: 30 minutes | Cook time: 4 minutes per batch | Serves 4

Meat:
- 4 garlic cloves, minced
- 2 teaspoons soy sauce
- 2 teaspoons sugar
- 1 teaspoon toasted sesame oil

Salad:
- 2 tablespoons rice vinegar or apple cider vinegar
- 2 tablespoons vegetable oil
- 1 garlic clove, minced
- 2 teaspoons sugar
- ¼ teaspoon coarse or flaky salt
- ¼ teaspoon black pepper

For Serving:
- Lime wedges
- Coarse salt and freshly cracked black pepper, to taste

- 1 teaspoon coarse or flaky salt
- ¼ teaspoon black pepper
- 680 g flat iron or top rump steak, cut into 1-inch cubes

- ½ red onion, halved and very thinly sliced
- 1 head butterhead lettuce, leaves separated and torn into large pieces
- 120 g halved baby plum tomatoes
- 60 g fresh mint leaves

1. For the meat: In a small bowl, combine the garlic, soy sauce, sugar, sesame oil, salt, and pepper. Place the meat in a gallon-size resealable plastic bag. Pour the marinade over the meat. Seal and place the bag in a large bowl. Marinate for 30 minutes, or cover and refrigerate for up to 24 hours. 2. Place half the meat in the air fryer basket. Set the air fryer to 230°C for 4 minutes, shaking the basket to redistribute the meat halfway through the cooking time. Transfer the meat to a plate (it should be medium-rare, still pink in the middle). Cover lightly with aluminium foil. Repeat to cook the remaining meat. 3. Meanwhile, for the salad: In a large bowl, whisk together the vinegar, vegetable oil, garlic, sugar, salt, and pepper. Add the onion. Stir to combine. Add the lettuce, tomatoes, and mint and toss to combine. Arrange the salad on a serving platter. 4. Arrange the cooked meat over the salad. Drizzle any accumulated juices from the plate over the meat. Serve with lime wedges, coarse salt, and cracked black pepper.

Saucy Beef Fingers

Prep time: 30 minutes | Cook time: 14 minutes | Serves 4

- 680 g rump steak
- 60 ml red wine
- 60 g fresh lime juice
- 1 teaspoon garlic powder
- 1 teaspoon onion granules
- 1 teaspoon celery salt
- 1 teaspoon mustard seeds
- Coarse sea salt and ground black pepper, to taste
- 1 teaspoon red pepper flakes
- 2 eggs, lightly whisked
- 235 g Parmesan cheese
- 1 teaspoon paprika

1. Combine the steak, red wine, lime juice, garlic powder, onion granules, celery salt, mustard seeds, salt, black pepper, and red pepper in a large ceramic bowl. Mix thoroughly to coat the steak evenly. Cover and marinate in the refrigerator for 3 hours to infuse the flavors.2. After marinating, tenderize the steak by gently pounding it with a mallet to break down the fibers. Slice the steak into 1-inch wide strips for easy cooking.3. Prepare the coating by whisking the eggs in a shallow bowl. In a separate bowl, mix Parmesan cheese and paprika to create a flavorful dredge.4. Dip each steak strip into the whisked eggs, ensuring it's well coated, then roll it in the Parmesan mixture, pressing gently to adhere the coating.5. Arrange the coated steak strips in the air fryer basket, leaving space between them for even cooking. Set the air fryer to 200°C and cook for 14 minutes, flipping halfway through to achieve a golden, crispy texture on all sides.6. While the steak fingers cook, prepare the dipping sauce by pouring the reserved marinade into a saucepan. Heat it over medium heat and let it simmer until warm and slightly thickened.7. Once the steak fingers are ready, transfer them to a serving plate and serve immediately with the warmed sauce on the side for dipping. Enjoy the tender and flavorful steak fingers!

Zesty Lime-Pepper Steak Stir

Prep time: 30 minutes | Cook time: 20 to 23 minutes | Serves 6

- 60 ml avocado oil
- 60 g freshly squeezed lime juice
- 2 teaspoons minced garlic
- 1 tablespoon chilli powder
- ½ teaspoon ground cumin
- Sea salt and freshly ground black pepper, to taste
- 450 g top rump steak or bavette or skirt steak, thinly sliced against the grain
- 1 red pepper, cored, seeded, and cut into ½-inch slices
- 1 green pepper, cored, seeded, and cut into ½-inch slices
- 1 large onion, sliced

1. In a small bowl or blender, combine the avocado oil, lime juice, garlic, chilli powder, cumin, and salt and pepper to taste. 2. Place the sliced steak in a zip-top bag or shallow dish. Place the peppers and onion in a separate zip-top bag or dish. Pour half the marinade over the steak and the other half over the vegetables. Seal both bags and let the steak and vegetables marinate in the refrigerator for at least 1 hour or up to 4 hours. 3. Line the air fryer basket with an air fryer liner or aluminium foil. Remove the vegetables from their bag or dish and shake off any excess marinade. Set the air fryer to 200°C. Place the vegetables in the air fryer basket and cook for 13 minutes. 4. Remove the steak from its bag or dish and shake off any excess marinade. Place the steak on top of the vegetables in the air fryer, and cook for 7 to 10 minutes or until an instant-read thermometer reads 49°C for medium-rare (or cook to your desired doneness). 5. Serve with desired fixings, such as keto maize wraps, lettuce, sour cream, avocado slices, shredded Cheddar cheese, and coriander.

Savory Garlic Steak Nuggets

Prep time: 5 minutes | Cook time: 16 minutes | Serves 3

- Oil, for spraying
- 450 g boneless steak, cut into 1-inch pieces
- 2 tablespoons olive oil
- 1 teaspoon Worcestershire sauce
- ½ teaspoon granulated garlic
- ½ teaspoon salt
- ¼ teaspoon freshly ground black pepper

1. Preheat the air fryer to 200°C. Line the air fryer basket with parchment and spray lightly with oil. 2. In a medium bowl, combine the steak, olive oil, Worcestershire sauce, garlic, salt, and black pepper and toss until evenly coated. 3. Place the steak in a single layer in the prepared basket. You may have to work in batches, depending on the size of your air fryer. 4. Cook for 10 to 16 minutes, flipping every 3 to 4 minutes. The total cooking time will depend on the thickness of the meat and your preferred doneness. If you want it well done, it may take up to 5 additional minutes.

Pork Loin with Aloha Salsa

Prep time: 20 minutes | Cook time: 7 to 9 minutes | Serves 4

Aloha Salsa:

- 235 g fresh pineapple, chopped in small pieces
- 60 g red onion, finely chopped
- 60 g green or red pepper, chopped
- ½ teaspoon ground cinnamon
- 1 teaspoon reduced-salt soy sauce
- ⅛ teaspoon crushed red pepper
- ⅛ teaspoon ground black pepper
- 2 eggs
- 2 tablespoons milk
- 30 g flour
- 30 g panko bread crumbs
- 4 teaspoons sesame seeds
- 450 g boneless, thin pork loin or tenderloin (⅜ to ½-inch thick)
- Pepper and salt
- 30 g cornflour
- Oil for misting or cooking spray

1. In a medium bowl, combine all the ingredients for the salsa, mixing well to ensure the flavors blend. Cover the bowl and refrigerate the salsa to keep it fresh while you prepare the pork.2. Preheat the air fryer to 200°C to ensure it's hot and ready for cooking.3. In a shallow dish, whisk together the eggs and milk until smooth to create an egg wash.4. In a separate shallow dish, mix the flour, panko breadcrumbs, and sesame seeds to make the coating for the pork.5. Season the pork cutlets with salt and pepper on both sides according to taste.6. Dredge each pork cutlet in cornflour, then dip it into the egg mixture, and finally coat it evenly with the panko and sesame seed mixture. Lightly spray both sides of the coated pork with oil or cooking spray for a crisp finish.7. Place the cutlets in the air fryer and cook for 3 minutes. Flip them over, spray both sides again, and continue cooking for an additional 4 to 6 minutes, or until the pork is golden and fully cooked through.8. Serve the crispy pork cutlets immediately with the chilled salsa on the side for a refreshing, flavorful accompaniment.

Chapter 7

Snacks and Starters

Chapter 7 Snacks and Starters

Spicy Chicken Bites

Prep time: 10 minutes | Cook time: 10 to 12 minutes | Makes 30 bites

- 227 g boneless and skinless chicken thighs, cut into 30 pieces
- ¼ teaspoon rock salt
- 2 tablespoons hot sauce
- Cooking spray

1. Begin by preheating the air fryer to 200ºC to ensure it's ready for cooking.2. Lightly spray the air fryer basket with cooking spray to prevent sticking. Season the chicken bites generously with rock salt and arrange them in a single layer in the basket. Air fry for 10 to 12 minutes, shaking the basket halfway through, until the bites are crispy and golden brown.3. While the chicken bites are cooking, pour the hot sauce into a large mixing bowl to prepare for coating.4. Once the chicken bites are done, transfer them directly into the bowl with the hot sauce. Toss thoroughly to ensure every piece is evenly coated. Serve immediately while warm and enjoy the crispy, flavorful bites!

Crispy Herbed Lentil Rice Bites

Prep time: 5 minutes | Cook time: 11 minutes | Serves 6

- 120 ml cooked green lentils
- 2 garlic cloves, minced
- ¼ white onion, minced
- 60 ml parsley leaves
- 5 basil leaves
- 235 ml cooked brown rice
- 1 tablespoon lemon juice
- 1 tablespoon olive oil
- ½ teaspoon salt

1. Preheat the air fryer to 192ºC. 2. In a food processor, pulse the cooked lentils with the garlic, onion, parsley, and basil until mostly smooth. (You will want some bits of lentils in the mixture.) Pour the lentil mixture into a large bowl, and stir in brown rice, lemon juice, olive oil, and salt. Stir until well combined. 3. Form the rice mixture into 1-inch balls. 4. Place the rice balls in a single layer in the air fryer basket, making sure that they don't touch each other. 5. Fry for 6 minutes. 6.Turn the rice balls and then fry for an additional 4 to 5 minutes, or until browned on all sides.

Crispy Lemony Pear Chips

Prep time: 15 minutes | Cook time: 9 to 13 minutes | Serves 4

- 2 firm Bosc or Anjou pears, cut crosswise into ⅛-inch-thick slices
- 1 tablespoon freshly squeezed lemon juice
- ½ teaspoon cinnamon powder
- ⅛ teaspoon ground cardamom

1. Preheat the air fryer to 190ºC. 2. Separate the smaller stem-end pear rounds from the larger rounds with seeds. Remove the core and seeds from the larger slices. Sprinkle all slices with lemon juice, cinnamon, and cardamom. 3. Put the smaller crisps into the air fryer basket. Air fry for 3 to 5 minutes, or until light golden, shaking the basket once during cooking. Remove from the air fryer. 4. Repeat with the larger slices, air frying for 6 to 8 minutes, or until light golden, shaking the basket once during cooking. 5. Remove the crisps from the air fryer. Cool and serve or store in an airtight container at room temperature up for to 2 days.

Crunchy Basil White Beans

Prep time: 2 minutes | Cook time: 19 minutes | Serves 2

- 1 (425 g) tin cooked white beans
- 2 tablespoons olive oil
- 1 teaspoon fresh sage, chopped
- ¼ teaspoon garlic powder
- ¼ teaspoon salt, divided
- 1 teaspoon chopped fresh basil

1. Start by preheating the air fryer to 190ºC to ensure even cooking.2. In a medium-sized bowl, combine the white beans, olive oil, chopped sage, minced garlic, ⅛ teaspoon salt, and dried basil. Mix thoroughly to coat the beans evenly with the seasonings.3. Transfer the seasoned beans to the air fryer basket, spreading them out in a single layer to promote crispiness.4. Cook the beans in the air fryer for 10 minutes, then give them a stir to ensure even cooking. Continue air frying for an additional 5 to 9 minutes, depending on your desired level of crunchiness.5. Once cooked, sprinkle the beans with the remaining ⅛ teaspoon salt and toss gently. Serve immediately for a flavorful and crispy snack.

Beef and Mango Skewers

Prep time: 10 minutes | Cook time: 4 to 7 minutes | Serves 4

- 340 g beef sirloin tip, cut into 1-inch cubes
- 2 tablespoons balsamic vinegar
- 1 tablespoon olive oil
- 1 tablespoon honey
- ½ teaspoon dried marjoram
- Pinch of salt
- Freshly ground black pepper, to taste
- 1 mango

1. Preheat the air fryer to 200°C to ensure it's ready for cooking. 2. Place the beef cubes in a medium-sized bowl and add the balsamic vinegar, olive oil, honey, marjoram, salt, and pepper. Mix everything thoroughly, then massage the marinade into the beef cubes with your hands to ensure they are evenly coated. Set the marinated beef aside to allow the flavors to absorb. 3. To prepare the mango, stand it upright and use a sharp knife to remove the skin. Carefully cut around the pit to remove the flesh, then chop the mango into 1-inch cubes. 4. Thread the beef and mango onto metal skewers, alternating between three beef cubes and two mango cubes for a balanced combination of savory and sweet. 5. Place the skewers in the air fryer basket and cook for 4 to 7 minutes, or until the beef is browned and reaches an internal temperature of at least 63°C. 6. Once cooked, remove the skewers from the air fryer and serve hot for a delicious and flavorful meal.

Creamy Greek Yogurt Deviled Eggs

Prep time: 15 minutes | Cook time: 15 minutes | Serves 4

- 4 eggs
- 60 ml non-fat plain Greek yoghurt
- 1 teaspoon chopped fresh fresh dill
- ⅛ teaspoon salt
- ⅛ teaspoon paprika
- ⅛ teaspoon garlic powder
- Chopped fresh parsley, for garnish

1. Preheat the air fryer to 130°C. 2. Place the eggs in a single layer in the air fryer basket and cook for 15 minutes. 3. Quickly remove the eggs from the air fryer and place them into a cold water bath. Let the eggs cool in the water for 10 minutes before removing and peeling them. 4. After peeling the eggs, cut them in half. 5. Spoon the yolk into a small bowl. Add the yoghurt, fresh dill, salt, paprika, and garlic powder and mix until smooth. 6. Spoon or pipe the yolk mixture into the halved egg whites. Serve with a sprinkle of fresh parsley on top.

Crispy Air-Fried Mozzarella Arancini

Prep time: 5 minutes | Cook time: 30 minutes | Makes 10 arancini

- 160 g raw white Arborio rice
- 2 teaspoons butter
- ½ teaspoon salt
- 315 ml water
- 2 large eggs, well beaten
- 150 g dried breadcrumbs mixed with Italian-style seasoning
- 10 ¾-inch semi-firm Mozzarella cubes
- Cooking spray

1. Pour the rice, butter, salt, and water in a pot 2. Stir to mix well and bring a boil over medium-high heat 3. Keep stirring 4. Reduce the heat to low and cover the pot 5. Simmer for 20 minutes or until the rice is tender 6. Turn off the heat and let sit, covered, for 10 minutes, then open the lid and fluffy the rice with a fork 7. Allow to cool for 10 more minutes 8. Preheat the air fryer to 190°C 9. Pour the beaten eggs in a bowl, then pour the breadcrumbs in a separate bowl 10. Scoop 2 tablespoons of the cooked rice up and form it into a ball, then press the Mozzarella into the ball and wrap 11. Dredge the ball in the eggs first, then shake the excess off the dunk the ball in the breadcrumbs 12. Roll to coat evenly 13. Repeat to make 10 balls in total with remaining rice 14. Transfer the balls in the preheated air fryer and spritz with cooking spray 15. You need to work in batches to avoid overcrowding 16. Air fry for 10 minutes or until the balls are lightly browned and crispy 17. Remove the balls from the air fryer and allow to cool before serving.

Golden Crispy Air-Fried Latkes

Prep time: 15 minutes | Cook time: 10 minutes | Makes 4 latkes

- 1 egg
- 2 tablespoons plain flour
- 2 medium potatoes, peeled and shredded, rinsed and drained
- ¼ teaspoon granulated garlic
- ½ teaspoon salt
- Cooking spray

1. Preheat the air fryer to 190°C 2. Spritz the air fryer basket with cooking spray 3. Whisk together the egg, flour, potatoes, garlic, and salt in a large bowl 4. Stir to mix well 5. Divide the mixture into four parts, then flatten them into four circles 6. Arrange the circles into the preheated air fryer 7. Spritz the circles with cooking spray, then air fry for 10 minutes or until golden brown and crispy 8. Flip the latkes halfway through 9. Serve immediately.

Crispy Sweet Potato Fries with Spicy Mayo Dip

Prep time: 5 minutes | Cook time: 20 minutes | Serves 2 to 3

- 1 large sweet potato (about 450 g), scrubbed
- 1 teaspoon mixed vegetables

Dipping Sauce:
- 60 ml light mayonnaise
- ½ teaspoon sriracha sauce
- 1 tablespoon spicy brown mustard
- 1 tablespoon sweet Thai chilli sauce
- or rapeseed oil
- Salt, to taste

1. Preheat the air fryer to 90ºC. 2. On a flat work surface, cut the sweet potato into fry-shaped strips about ¼ inch wide and ¼ inch thick. You tin use a mandoline to slice the sweet potato quickly and uniformly. 3. In a medium-sized bowl, drizzle the sweet potato strips with the oil and toss well. 4. Transfer to the air fryer basket and air fry for 10 minutes, shaking the basket twice during cooking. 5. Remove the air fryer basket and sprinkle with the salt and toss to coat. 6. Increase the air fryer temperature to 200ºC and air fry for an additional 10 minutes, or until the fries are crispy and tender. Shake the basket a few times during cooking. 7. Meanwhile, whisk together all the ingredients for the sauce in a small bowl. 8. Remove the sweet potato fries from the basket to a plate and serve warm alongside the dipping sauce.

Crispy Filo Artichoke Triangles

Prep time: 15 minutes | Cook time: 9 to 12 minutes | Makes 18 triangles

- 70 g Ricotta cheese
- 1 egg white
- 60 g minced and drained artichoke hearts
- 3 tablespoons grated mozzarella cheese cheese
- ½ teaspoon dried thyme
- 6 sheets frozen filo pastry, thawed
- 2 tablespoons melted butter

1. Preheat the air fryer to 200ºC to ensure it's hot and ready for baking.2. In a small bowl, combine the Ricotta cheese, egg white, chopped artichoke hearts, mozzarella cheese, and thyme. Mix everything together until smooth and well combined.3. Keep the filo pastry covered with a damp kitchen towel to prevent it from drying out while you work. Take one sheet of filo at a time, lay it flat on the work surface, and cut it into thirds lengthwise.4. Place about 1½ teaspoons of the cheese and artichoke filling at the base of each strip. Fold the bottom right-hand corner of the filo over the filling to form a triangle, then continue folding in a triangle shape until the entire strip is rolled up. Brush the edges with butter to seal them. Repeat with the remaining filo and filling.5. Arrange the filled triangles in the air fryer basket, placing no more than 6 at a time to allow room for crisping. Bake for 3 to 4 minutes, or until the filo is golden brown and crisp.6. Serve the crispy artichoke triangles hot for a delicious, savory snack or appetizer.

Healthy Veggie Salmon Nachos

Prep time: 10 minutes | Cook time: 9 to 12 minutes | Serves 6

- 57 g baked no-salt sweetcorn tortilla chips
- 1 (142 g) baked salmon fillet, flaked
- 100 g canned low-salt black beans, rinsed and drained
- 1 red pepper, chopped
- 50 g grated carrot
- 1 jalapeño chillies pepper, minced
- 30 g shredded low-salt low-fat Swiss cheese
- 1 tomato, chopped

1. Preheat the air fryer to 180ºC. 2. In a baking pan, layer the tortilla chips. Top with the salmon, black beans, red pepper, carrot, jalapeño chillies, and Swiss cheese. 3. Bake in the air fryer for 9 to 12 minutes, or until the cheese is melted and starts to brown. 4. Top with the tomato and serve.

Greens Crisps with Curried Yoghurt Sauce

Prep time: 10 minutes | Cook time: 5 to 6 minutes | Serves 4

- 240 ml low-fat Greek yoghurt
- 1 tablespoon freshly squeezed lemon juice
- 1 tablespoon curry powder
- ½ bunch curly kale, stemmed, ribs removed and discarded, leaves cut into 2- to 3-inch pieces
- ½ bunch chard, stemmed, ribs removed and discarded, leaves cut into 2- to 3-inch pieces
- 1½ teaspoons olive oil

1. In a small bowl, combine the yoghurt, lemon juice, and curry powder, stirring until smooth. Set the sauce aside to allow the flavors to meld.2. In a large bowl, add the kale and chard, then drizzle with olive oil. Use your hands to massage the oil into the leaves, ensuring each leaf is evenly coated. This helps break down the fibers, making the crisps tender and flavorful.3. Preheat the air fryer to 200ºC. Cook the greens in batches by placing them in the air fryer basket in a single layer. Air fry for 5 to 6 minutes, shaking the basket halfway through, until the greens are crispy.4. Serve the crispy kale and chard with the prepared yoghurt sauce for dipping. Enjoy the light and flavorful snack!

Rosemary-Garlic Shoestring Fries

Prep time: 5 minutes | Cook time: 18 minutes | Serves 2

- 1 large russet potatoes or Maris Piper potato (about 340 g), scrubbed clean, and julienned
- 1 tablespoon mixed vegetables oil
- Leaves from 1 sprig fresh rosemary
- Rock salt and freshly ground black pepper, to taste
- 1 garlic clove, thinly sliced
- Flaky sea salt, for serving

1. Preheat the air fryer to 200°C to ensure it's hot and ready for cooking. 2. Place the julienned potatoes in a large colander and rinse them thoroughly under cold running water until the water runs clear, removing excess starch. Lay the potatoes out on a double layer of kitchen roll and pat them dry to ensure they crisp up well during cooking. 3. In a large bowl, combine the dried potatoes with oil and rosemary. Season generously with rock salt and pepper, then toss everything together to coat the potatoes evenly. Arrange the seasoned potatoes in the air fryer basket and cook for 18 minutes, shaking the basket every 5 minutes to ensure even cooking. Add minced garlic during the last 5 minutes of cooking to infuse flavor. 4. Once the fries are golden and crispy, transfer them to a serving plate. While they're still hot, sprinkle with flaky sea salt for extra flavor. Serve immediately and enjoy your perfectly crispy fries!

Kale Salad Sushi Rolls with Sriracha Mayonnaise

Prep time: 10 minutes | Cook time: 10 minutes | Serves 12

Kale Salad:
- 350 g chopped kale
- 1 tablespoon sesame seeds
- ¾ teaspoon soy sauce
- ¾ teaspoon toasted sesame oil
- ½ teaspoon rice vinegar
- ¼ teaspoon ginger
- ⅛ teaspoon garlic powder

Sushi Rolls:
- 3 sheets sushi nori
- 1 batch cauliflower rice
- ½ avocado, sliced

Coating:
- 60 g panko breadcrumbs

Sriracha Mayonnaise:
- 60 ml Sriracha sauce
- 60 ml vegan mayonnaise

1. Preheat the air fryer to 200°C to ensure it's fully heated for cooking. 2. In a medium bowl, toss all the ingredients for the kale salad together until everything is well coated. Set the salad aside to allow the flavors to meld. 3. Lay a sheet of nori on a clean surface and evenly spread the cauliflower rice over it, creating a thin layer. 4. Scoop 2 to 3 tablespoons of the kale salad and spread it evenly over the rice. 5. Add 1 or 2 slices of avocado on top of the kale salad for added creaminess. 6. Carefully roll up the sushi, pressing gently as you go to create a tight and secure roll. 7. Repeat the process with the remaining ingredients to make two more rolls. 8. In a separate bowl, mix together the Sriracha sauce and mayonnaise until smooth and well combined. 9. Pour breadcrumbs into another bowl, ready for coating. 10. Dip each sushi roll into the Sriracha mayonnaise, ensuring it's well coated, then roll it in the breadcrumbs for a crunchy exterior. 11. Place the coated sushi rolls in the air fryer basket, ensuring they are not overcrowded. Air fry for 10 minutes, or until the rolls are golden brown and crispy. 12. Flip the sushi rolls gently halfway through the cooking time to ensure even crispiness on all sides. 13. After cooking, transfer the rolls to a platter and let them rest for 5 minutes before slicing each roll into 8 pieces. 14. Serve the sushi warm, and enjoy a crispy, flavorful treat!

Classic Air-Fried Scotch Eggs

Prep time: 15 minutes | Cook time: 11 to 13 minutes | Serves 6

- 680 g bulk lean chicken or turkey banger
- 3 raw eggs, divided
- 100 g dried breadcrumbs, divided
- 65 g plain flour
- 6 hardboiled eggs, peeled
- Cooking oil spray

1. In a large bowl, combine the chicken banger, 1 raw egg, and 40 g of breadcrumbs and mix well. Divide the mixture into 6 pieces and flatten each into a long oval. 2. In a shallow dish, beat the remaining 2 raw eggs. 3. Place the flour in a small bowl. 4. Place the remaining 80 g of breadcrumbs in a second small bowl. 5. Roll each hardboiled egg in the flour and wrap one of the chicken banger pieces around each egg to encircle it completely. 6. One at a time, roll the encased eggs in the flour, dip in the beaten eggs, and finally dip in the breadcrumbs to coat. 7. Insert the crisper plate into the basket and the basket into the unit. Preheat the unit by selecting AIR FRY, setting the temperature to 190°C, and setting the time to 3 minutes. Select START/STOP to begin. 8. Once the unit is preheated, spray the crisper plate with cooking oil. Place the eggs in a single layer into the basket and spray them with oil. 9. Select AIR FRY, set the temperature to 190°C, and set the time to 13 minutes. Select START/STOP to begin. 10. After about 6 minutes, use tongs to turn the eggs and spray them with more oil. Resume cooking for 5 to 7 minutes more, or until the chicken is thoroughly cooked and the Scotch eggs are browned. 11. When the cooking is complete, serve warm.

Chilli-brined Fried Calamari

Prep time: 20 minutes | Cook time: 8 minutes | Serves 2

- 1 (227 g) jar sweet or hot pickled cherry peppers
- 227 g calamari bodies and tentacles, bodies cut into ½-inch-wide rings
- 1 lemon
- 200 g plain flour
- Rock salt and freshly ground black pepper, to taste
- 3 large eggs, lightly beaten
- Cooking spray
- 120 ml mayonnaise
- 1 teaspoon finely chopped rosemary
- 1 garlic clove, minced

1. Begin by draining the pickled pepper brine into a large bowl, then tear the pickled peppers into bite-sized strips. Add the pepper strips and calamari to the brine, stirring to coat. Let the mixture marinate in the refrigerator for 20 minutes to 2 hours to infuse the flavors.2. Grate the zest from the lemon into a large bowl, then whisk in the flour. Season the mixture with salt and pepper to taste. Dip the marinated calamari and pepper strips into the beaten egg, ensuring they are fully coated, then toss them in the seasoned flour mixture until well-coated.3. Spray the battered calamari and peppers generously with cooking spray to help them crisp up. Place half of the mixture into the air fryer basket and cook at 200ºC, shaking the basket halfway through the cooking time. Air fry for about 8 minutes, or until the calamari is golden and fully cooked. Transfer to a plate and repeat the process with the remaining pieces.4. While the calamari and peppers are cooking, prepare the dipping sauce. In a small bowl, whisk together mayonnaise, finely chopped rosemary, and minced garlic. Squeeze the juice from half of the zested lemon (about 1 tablespoon) into the sauce and stir to combine. Season with salt and pepper to taste.5. Cut the remaining half of the zested lemon into four small wedges. Serve the crispy calamari and peppers with the lemon wedges and rosemary-garlic dipping sauce on the side. Enjoy!

Lemony Curried Endive with Yogurt Marinade

Prep time: 5 minutes | Cook time: 10 minutes | Serves 6

- 6 heads endive
- 120 ml plain and fat-free yoghurt
- 3 tablespoons lemon juice
- 1 teaspoon garlic powder
- ½ teaspoon curry powder
- Salt and ground black pepper, to taste

1. Wash the endives and slice them in half lengthwise. 2. In a bowl, mix together the yoghurt, lemon juice, garlic powder, curry powder, salt and pepper. 3. Brush the endive halves with the marinade, coating them completely. Allow to sit for at least 30 minutes or up to 24 hours. 4. Preheat the air fryer to 160ºC. 5. Put the endives in the air fryer basket and air fry for 10 minutes. 6. Serve hot.

Classic Spring Rolls

Prep time: 10 minutes | Cook time: 9 minutes | Makes 16 spring rolls

- 4 teaspoons toasted sesame oil
- 6 medium garlic cloves, minced or pressed
- 1 tablespoon grated peeled fresh ginger
- 70 g thinly sliced shiitake mushrooms
- 500 g chopped green cabbage
- 80 g grated carrot
- ½ teaspoon sea salt
- 16 rice paper wrappers
- Cooking oil spray (sunflower, safflower, or refined coconut)
- Gluten-free sweet and sour sauce or Thai sweet chilli sauce, for serving (optional)

1. Begin by placing a wok or sauté pan over medium heat until it becomes hot.2. Add sesame oil, minced garlic, grated ginger, sliced mushrooms, shredded cabbage, grated carrot, and a pinch of salt to the pan. Cook for 3 to 4 minutes, stirring frequently, until the cabbage starts to wilt slightly. Remove the pan from the heat once the vegetables are tender.3. Gently dip a rice paper wrapper under water until it softens. Lay it flat on a non-absorbent surface. Place about 30g of the cabbage filling in the center of the wrapper. Once the wrapper is pliable, fold the bottom up over the filling, then fold in the sides, and roll the wrapper tightly to encase the filling, similar to making a small burrito.4. Repeat the rolling process for the remaining rice papers, using the cabbage mixture until you've prepared the desired number of spring rolls. Ensure they fit in the air fryer basket in a single layer, leaving some space between them. Refrigerate any leftover filling in an airtight container for up to a week.5. Insert the crisper plate into the air fryer basket, then place the basket in the unit. Preheat the air fryer by selecting the AIR FRY option, setting the temperature to 200ºC, and the time to 3 minutes. Press START/STOP to begin preheating.6. Once the unit has preheated, lightly spray both the crisper plate and the basket with cooking oil. Arrange the spring rolls in the basket, ensuring there is enough space between them to prevent sticking. Spray the top of each spring roll with a light layer of cooking oil.7. Select the AIR FRY option again, set the temperature to 200ºC, and set the time to 9 minutes. Press START/STOP to begin cooking.8. Once the cooking cycle is complete, the spring rolls should be crispy and lightly browned. Serve immediately, either plain or with your preferred dipping sauce. Enjoy!

Crispy String Bean Fries

Prep time: 15 minutes | Cook time: 5 to 6 minutes | Serves 4

- 227 g fresh French beans
- 2 eggs
- 4 teaspoons water
- 60 g plain flour
- 50 g breadcrumbs
- ¼ teaspoon salt
- ¼ teaspoon ground black pepper
- ¼ teaspoon mustard powder (optional)
- Oil for misting or cooking spray

1. Preheat the air fryer to 180°C. 2. Trim stem ends from French beans, wash, and pat dry. 3. In a shallow dish, beat eggs and water together until well blended. 4. Place flour in a second shallow dish. 5. In a third shallow dish, stir together the breadcrumbs, salt, pepper, and mustard powder if using. 6. Dip each bean in egg mixture, flour, egg mixture again, then breadcrumbs. 7. When you finish coating all the French beans, open air fryer and place them in basket. 8. Cook for 3 minutes. 9. Stop and mist French beans with oil or cooking spray. 10. Cook for 2 to 3 more minutes or until French beans are crispy and nicely browned.

Five-Ingredient Falafel with Garlic-Yoghurt Sauce

Prep time: 5 minutes | Cook time: 15 minutes | Serves 4

Falafel:
- 1 (425 g) tin chickpeas, drained and rinsed
- 30 g fresh parsley
- 2 garlic cloves, minced

Garlic-Yoghurt Sauce:
- 240 ml non-fat plain Greek yoghurt
- 1 garlic clove, minced
- ½ tablespoon cumin powder
- 1 tablespoon wholemeal flour
- Salt
- 1 tablespoon chopped fresh fresh dill
- 2 tablespoons lemon juice

Make the Falafel: 1. Preheat the air fryer to 180°C, ensuring it's hot and ready for cooking. 2. Place the chickpeas into a food processor and pulse until they are mostly chopped. Add the parsley, garlic, and cumin, then pulse for another 1 to 2 minutes until the mixture starts coming together into a dough-like texture. 3. Add the flour and pulse a few more times to combine. The dough should have texture, with small bits of chickpeas still visible. 4. Using your hands, roll the dough into 8 equal-sized balls, then gently flatten each ball into a disk about ½-inch thick. 5. Lightly spray the air fryer basket with olive oil cooking spray. Place the falafel patties in the basket in a single layer, ensuring they are not touching each other. 6. Air fry the falafel for 15 minutes, or until they are golden brown and crispy on all sides.

Make the Garlic-Yogurt Sauce: 7. In a small bowl, combine the yoghurt, minced garlic, fresh dill, and lemon juice. Stir until smooth and well mixed. 8. Once the falafel is cooked and nicely browned, remove them from the air fryer. Season with a pinch of salt to taste. 9. Serve the falafel hot with the garlic-yoghurt dipping sauce on the side for a delicious and flavorful meal.

Crispy Prawn Egg Rolls

Prep time: 15 minutes | Cook time: 10 minutes per batch | Serves 4

- 1 tablespoon mixed vegetables oil
- ½ head green or savoy cabbage, finely shredded
- 90 g grated carrots
- 240 ml canned bean sprouts, drained
- 1 tablespoon soy sauce
- ½ teaspoon sugar
- 1 teaspoon sesame oil
- 60 ml hoisin sauce
- Freshly ground black pepper, to taste
- 454 g cooked prawns, diced
- 30 g spring onions
- 8 egg roll wrappers (or use spring roll pastry)
- mixed vegetables oil
- Duck sauce

1. Preheat a large sauté pan over medium-high heat. Add the oil and cook the cabbage, carrots and bean sprouts until they start to wilt, about 3 minutes. Add the soy sauce, sugar, sesame oil, hoisin sauce and black pepper. Sauté for a few more minutes. Stir in the prawns and spring onions and cook until the mixed vegetables are just tender. Transfer the mixture to a colander in a bowl to cool. Press or squeeze out any excess water from the filling so that you don't end up with soggy egg rolls. 2. Make the egg rolls: Place the egg roll wrappers on a flat surface with one of the points facing towards you so they look like diamonds. Dividing the filling evenly between the eight wrappers, spoon the mixture onto the centre of the egg roll wrappers. Spread the filling across the centre of the wrappers from the left corner to the right corner but leave 2 inches from each corner empty. Brush the empty sides of the wrapper with a little water. Fold the bottom corner of the wrapper tightly up over the filling, trying to avoid making any air pockets. Fold the left corner in toward the centre and then the right corner toward the centre. It should now look like an packet. Tightly roll the egg roll from the bottom to the top open corner. Press to seal the egg roll together, brushing with a little extra water if need be. Repeat this technique with all 8 egg rolls. 3. Preheat the air fryer to 190°C. 4. Spray or brush all sides of the egg rolls with mixed vegetables oil. Air fry four egg rolls at a time for 10 minutes, turning them over halfway through the cooking time. 5. Serve hot with duck sauce or your favourite dipping sauce.

Roasted Mushrooms with Garlic

Prep time: 3 minutes | Cook time: 22 to 27 minutes | Serves 4

- 16 garlic cloves, peeled
- 2 teaspoons olive oil, divided
- 16 button mushrooms
- ½ teaspoon dried marjoram
- ⅛ teaspoon freshly ground black pepper
- 1 tablespoon white wine or low-salt mixed vegetables broth

1. Preheat your air fryer to 180°C. In a small bowl, combine crushed garlic and a teaspoon of olive oil. Spread the mixture evenly on a baking tray and place it in the air fryer. Cook for about 12 minutes, allowing the garlic to soften and become fragrant. 2. Meanwhile, clean and slice your mushrooms. After the garlic has roasted, add the mushrooms to the pan along with a sprinkle of marjoram and freshly cracked pepper. Toss everything to ensure the mushrooms are evenly coated. Drizzle the remaining olive oil and a splash of white wine over the top for added flavor. 3. Place the pan back in the air fryer and cook for another 10 to 15 minutes, or until the mushrooms are golden and tender, and the garlic has caramelized. Once done, serve immediately, enjoying the rich, roasted flavors.

Savory Mushroom and Gruyère Tarts

Prep time: 15 minutes | Cook time: 38 minutes | Makes 15 tarts

- 2 tablespoons extra-virgin olive oil, divided
- 1 small white onion, sliced
- 227 g shiitake mushrooms, sliced
- ¼ teaspoon sea salt
- ¼ teaspoon freshly ground black pepper
- 60 ml dry white wine
- 1 sheet frozen puff pastry, thawed
- 95 g shredded Gruyère cheese
- Cooking oil spray
- 1 tablespoon thinly sliced fresh chives

1. Insert the crisper plate into the basket and the basket into the unit. Preheat the unit by selecting BAKE, setting the temperature to 150°C, and setting the time to 3 minutes. Select START/STOP to begin. 2. In a heatproof bowl that fits into the basket, stir together 1 tablespoon of olive oil, the onion, and the mushrooms. 3. Once the unit is preheated, place the bowl into the basket. 4. Select BAKE, set the temperature to 150°C, and set the time to 7 minutes. Select START/STOP to begin. 5. After about 2½ minutes, stir the mixed vegetables. Resume cooking. After another 2½ minutes, the mixed vegetables should be browned and tender. Season with the salt and pepper and add the wine. Resume cooking until the liquid evaporates, about 2 minutes. 6. When the cooking is complete, place the bowl on a heatproof surface. 7. Increase the air fryer temperature to 200°C and set the time to 3 minutes. Select START/STOP to begin. 8. Unfold the puff pastry and cut it into 15 (3-by-3-inch) squares. Using a fork, pierce the dough and brush both sides with the remaining 1 tablespoon of olive oil. 9. Evenly distribute half the cheese among the puff pastry squares, leaving a ½-inch border around the edges. Divide the mushroom-onion mixture among the pastry squares and top with the remaining cheese. 10. Once the unit is preheated, spray the crisper plate with cooking oil. Working in batches, place 5 tarts into the basket; do not stack or overlap. 11. Select BAKE, set the temperature to 200°C, and set the time to 8 minutes. Select START/STOP to begin. 12. After 6 minutes, check the tarts; if not yet golden, resume cooking for about 2 minutes more. 13. When the cooking is complete, remove the tarts and transfer to a a wire rack to cool. Repeat steps 10, 11, and 12 with the remaining tarts. 14. Serve garnished with the chives.

Soft white cheese Stuffed Jalapeño Chillies Poppers

Prep time: 12 minutes | Cook time: 6 to 8 minutes | Serves 10

- 227 g soft white cheese, at room temperature
- 80 g panko breadcrumbs, divided
- 2 tablespoons fresh parsley, minced
- 1 teaspoon chilli powder
- 10 jalapeño chillies chillies, halved and seeded
- Cooking oil spray

1. Start by mixing soft white cheese, 40g of panko, parsley, and chili powder in a bowl until well blended. Carefully stuff the jalapeño halves with the cheese mixture, making sure each half is generously filled. 2. Sprinkle the remaining 40g of panko on top of the stuffed jalapeños, gently pressing it into the filling to ensure it sticks. 3. Prepare your air fryer by inserting the crisper plate into the basket, then place the basket inside the unit. Preheat the air fryer by selecting the AIR FRY setting, setting the temperature to 190°C, and adjusting the time to 3 minutes. Press START/STOP to begin preheating. 4. Once preheated, lightly spray the crisper plate with cooking oil to prevent sticking. Carefully arrange the stuffed poppers in the basket, making sure they are not overcrowded. 5. Set the air fryer to AIR FRY at 190°C for 8 minutes. Press START/STOP to start the cooking process. 6. After 6 minutes, check the poppers. If the cheese has melted and the poppers are tender, they are ready. If not, continue cooking until fully done. 7. Once cooked, serve the jalapeño poppers warm and enjoy the crispy, cheesy goodness.

Chapter 8

Vegetables and Sides

Chapter 8 Vegetables and Sides

Crispy Lemony Roasted Broccoli

Prep time: 10 minutes | Cook time: 9 to 14 minutes per batch | Serves 4

- 1 large head broccoli, rinsed and patted dry
- 2 teaspoons extra-virgin olive oil
- 1 tablespoon freshly squeezed lemon juice
- Olive oil spray

1. Cut off the broccoli florets and separate them. You tin use the stems, too; peel the stems and cut them into 1-inch chunks. 2. Insert the crisper plate into the basket and the basket into the unit. Preheat the unit by selecting AIR ROAST, setting the temperature to 200ºC, and setting the time to 3 minutes. Select START/STOP to begin. 3. In a large bowl, toss together the broccoli, olive oil, and lemon juice until coated. 4. Once the unit is preheated, spray the crisper plate with olive oil. Working in batches, place half the broccoli into the basket. 5. Select AIR ROAST, set the temperature to 200ºC, and set the time to 14 minutes. Select START/STOP to begin. 6. After 5 minutes, remove the basket and shake the broccoli. Reinsert the basket to resume cooking. Check the broccoli after 5 minutes. If it is crisp-tender and slightly brown around the edges, it is done. If not, resume cooking. 7. When the cooking is complete, transfer the broccoli to a serving bowl. Repeat steps 5 and 6 with the remaining broccoli. Serve immediately.

Courgette Fritters

Prep time: 10 minutes | Cook time: 10 minutes | Serves 4

- 2 courgette, grated (about 450 g)
- 1 teaspoon salt
- 25 g almond flour
- 20 g grated Parmesan cheese
- 1 large egg
- ¼ teaspoon dried thyme
- ¼ teaspoon ground turmeric
- ¼ teaspoon freshly ground black pepper
- 1 tablespoon olive oil

½ lemon, sliced into wedges

1. Begin by setting the air fryer to 200ºC to preheat. Cut a piece of parchment paper to fit just slightly smaller than the base of the air fryer basket, ensuring the paper will not obstruct airflow. 2. Place the courgette in a colander and sprinkle with salt. Let it rest for 5 to 10 minutes to draw out excess moisture. Afterward, squeeze out as much liquid as possible and transfer the courgette to a large mixing bowl. Add almond flour, grated Parmesan, an egg, thyme, turmeric, and black pepper. Mix gently but thoroughly until all ingredients are well combined. 3. Divide the mixture into 8 equal portions and form them into patties. Place them on the prepared parchment paper inside the air fryer basket. Lightly brush the tops of the patties with olive oil for a crispier finish. 4. Air fry the patties for about 10 minutes, flipping them halfway through the cooking process to ensure they are golden and crispy on both sides. Once done, serve the patties warm with fresh lemon wedges for an added zest.

Spicy Corn and Coriander Salad with Adobo Dressing

Prep time: 10 minutes | Cook time: 10 minutes | Serves 2

- 2 ears of maize, shucked (halved crosswise if too large to fit in your air fryer)
- 1 tablespoon unsalted butter, at room temperature
- 1 teaspoon chilli powder
- ¼ teaspoon garlic powder
- coarse sea salt and freshly ground black pepper, to taste
- 20 g lightly packed fresh coriander leaves
- 1 tablespoon sour cream
- 1 tablespoon mayonnaise
- 1 teaspoon adobo sauce (from a tin of chipotle peppers in adobo sauce)
- 2 tablespoons crumbled feta cheese
- Lime wedges, for serving

1. Brush the maize all over with the butter, then sprinkle with the chilli powder and garlic powder, and season with salt and pepper. Place the maize in the air fryer and air fry at 200ºC, turning over halfway through, until the kernels are lightly charred and tender, about 10 minutes. 2. Transfer the ears to a cutting board, let stand 1 minute, then carefully cut the kernels off the cobs and move them to a bowl. Add the coriander leaves and toss to combine (the coriander leaves will wilt slightly). 3. In a small bowl, stir together the sour cream, mayonnaise, and adobo sauce. Divide the maize and coriander among plates and spoon the adobo dressing over the top. Sprinkle with the feta cheese and serve with lime wedges on the side.

Crispy Roasted Potatoes with Asparagus Mash

Prep time: 5 minutes | Cook time: 23 minutes | Serves 4

- 4 medium potatoes
- 1 bunch asparagus
- 75 g cottage cheese
- 80 g low-fat crème fraiche
- 1 tablespoon wholegrain mustard
- Salt and pepper, to taste
- Cooking spray

1. Preheat the air fryer to 200ºC. Spritz the air fryer basket with cooking spray. 2. Place the potatoes in the basket. Air fry the potatoes for 20 minutes. 3. Boil the asparagus in salted water for 3 minutes. 4. Remove the potatoes and mash them with rest of ingredients. Sprinkle with salt and pepper. 5. Serve immediately.

Parmesan-Rosemary Radishes

Prep time: 5 minutes | Cook time: 15 to 20 minutes | Serves 4

- 1 bunch radishes, stemmed, trimmed, and quartered
- 1 tablespoon avocado oil
- 2 tablespoons finely grated fresh Parmesan cheese
- 1 tablespoon chopped fresh rosemary
- Sea salt and freshly ground black pepper, to taste

1. Begin by placing the radishes in a medium-sized bowl. Drizzle them with avocado oil and toss them to coat evenly. Add Parmesan cheese, rosemary, salt, and pepper, mixing everything together to ensure the radishes are well-seasoned. 2. Preheat the air fryer to 190ºC. Arrange the radishes in a single, even layer in the air fryer basket. Roast them for 15 to 20 minutes, allowing them to become golden and tender. 3. Once finished, let the roasted radishes cool for about 5 minutes before serving, allowing the flavors to set.

Maple-Roasted Tomatoes

Prep time: 15 minutes | Cook time: 20 minutes | Serves 2

- 280 g cherry tomatoes, halved
- coarse sea salt, to taste
- 2 tablespoons maple syrup
- 1 tablespoon vegetable oil
- 2 sprigs fresh thyme, stems removed
- 1 garlic clove, minced
- Freshly ground black pepper

1. Start by placing the tomatoes in a colander and generously sprinkling them with salt. Allow them to sit for 10 minutes to help draw out excess moisture. 2. Once drained, arrange the tomatoes cut-side up in a cake pan. Drizzle them with maple syrup and then with oil. Scatter thyme leaves and minced garlic over the tomatoes, and season with freshly cracked pepper. 3. Place the pan in the air fryer and set the temperature to 160ºC. Roast for approximately 20 minutes, until the tomatoes are tender, collapsed, and have developed a light caramelization on top. 4. Serve the tomatoes directly from the pan, or transfer them to a serving plate and drizzle with the flavorful juices from the pan for extra richness.

Garlic-Thyme Roasted Tomatoes

Prep time: 10 minutes | Cook time: 15 minutes | Serves 2 to 4

- 4 plum tomatoes
- 1 tablespoon olive oil
- Salt and freshly ground
- black pepper, to taste
- 1 clove garlic, minced
- ½ teaspoon dried thyme

1. Preheat the air fryer to 200ºC. 2. Cut the tomatoes in half and scoop out the seeds and any pithy parts with your fingers. Place the tomatoes in a bowl and toss with the olive oil, salt, pepper, garlic and thyme. 3. Transfer the tomatoes to the air fryer, cut side up. Air fry for 15 minutes. The edges should just start to brown. Let the tomatoes cool to an edible temperature for a few minutes and then use in pastas, on top of crostini, or as an accompaniment to any poultry, meat or fish.

Roasted Brussels Sprouts with Orange and Garlic

Prep time: 5 minutes | Cook time: 10 minutes | Serves 4

- 450 g Brussels sprouts, quartered
- 2 garlic cloves, minced
- 2 tablespoons olive oil
- ½ teaspoon salt
- 1 orange, cut into rings

1. Begin by preheating the air fryer to 180ºC. 2. In a large mixing bowl, combine the quartered Brussels sprouts with minced garlic, olive oil, and a pinch of salt. Toss everything together to ensure the Brussels sprouts are evenly coated. 3. Transfer the Brussels sprouts into the air fryer basket and place the orange slices on top. Roast for 10 minutes, allowing the flavors to meld and the sprouts to become tender. 4. Once done, remove from the air fryer and set the orange slices aside. Give the Brussels sprouts a final toss before serving to distribute the flavors evenly.

Crispy Brussels Sprouts with Toasted Pecans and Gorgonzola

Prep time: 10 minutes | Cook time: 25 minutes | Serves 4

- 65 g pecans
- 680 g fresh Brussels sprouts, trimmed and quartered
- 2 tablespoons olive oil
- Salt and freshly ground black pepper, to taste
- 30 g crumbled Gorgonzola cheese

1. Spread the pecans in a single layer of the air fryer and set the heat to 180°C. Air fry for 3 to 5 minutes until the pecans are lightly browned and fragrant. Transfer the pecans to a plate and continue preheating the air fryer, increasing the heat to 200°C. 2. In a large bowl, toss the Brussels sprouts with the olive oil and season with salt and black pepper to taste. 3. Working in batches if necessary, arrange the Brussels sprouts in a single layer in the air fryer basket. Pausing halfway through the baking time to shake the basket, air fry for 20 to 25 minutes until the sprouts are tender and starting to brown on the edges. 4. Transfer the sprouts to a serving bowl and top with the toasted pecans and Gorgonzola. Serve warm or at room temperature.

Honey-Sesame Carrots and Sugar Snap Peas

Prep time: 10 minutes | Cook time: 16 minutes | Serves 4

- 450 g carrots, peeled sliced on the bias (½-inch slices)
- 1 teaspoon olive oil
- Salt and freshly ground black pepper, to taste
- 110 g honey
- 1 tablespoon sesame oil
- 1 tablespoon soy sauce
- ½ teaspoon minced fresh ginger
- 110 g sugar snap peas
- 1½ teaspoons sesame seeds

1. Preheat the air fryer to 180°C. 2. Toss the carrots with the olive oil, season with salt and pepper and air fry for 10 minutes, shaking the basket once or twice during the cooking process. 3. Combine the honey, sesame oil, soy sauce and minced ginger in a large bowl. Add the sugar snap peas and the air-fried carrots to the honey mixture, toss to coat and return everything to the air fryer basket. 4. Turn up the temperature to 200°C and air fry for an additional 6 minutes, shaking the basket once during the cooking process. 5. Transfer the carrots and sugar snap peas to a serving bowl. Pour the sauce from the bottom of the cooker over the vegetables and sprinkle sesame seeds over top. Serve immediately.

Stuffed Ricotta Potatoes with Herbs and Cheese

Prep time: 15 minutes | Cook time: 15 minutes | Serves 4

- 4 potatoes
- 2 tablespoons olive oil
- 110 g Ricotta cheese, at room temperature
- 2 tablespoons chopped spring onions
- 1 tablespoon roughly chopped fresh parsley
- 1 tablespoon minced coriander
- 60 g Cheddar cheese, preferably freshly grated
- 1 teaspoon celery seeds
- ½ teaspoon salt
- ½ teaspoon garlic pepper

1. Preheat the air fryer to 180°C. 2. Pierce the skin of the potatoes with a knife. 3. Air fry in the air fryer basket for 13 minutes. If they are not cooked through by this time, leave for 2 to 3 minutes longer. 4. In the meantime, make the stuffing by combining all the other ingredients. 5. Cut halfway into the cooked potatoes to open them. 6. Spoon equal amounts of the stuffing into each potato and serve hot.

Fig, Chickpea, and Rocket Salad

Prep time: 15 minutes | Cook time: 20 minutes | Serves 4

- 8 fresh figs, halved
- 250 g cooked chickpeas
- 1 teaspoon crushed roasted cumin seeds
- 4 tablespoons balsamic vinegar
- 2 tablespoons extra-virgin olive oil, plus more for greasing
- Salt and ground black pepper, to taste
- 40 g rocket, washed and dried

1. Preheat the air fryer to 190°C. 2. Line the air fryer basket with aluminum foil and lightly grease it with oil to prevent sticking. Place the figs in the basket and air fry for 10 minutes. 3. While the figs are cooking, combine the chickpeas and cumin seeds in a bowl, mixing them together. 4. After the figs have finished air frying, remove them from the basket and add the chickpeas. Air fry the chickpeas for another 10 minutes, then set them aside to cool. 5. While the chickpeas cool, prepare the dressing by mixing balsamic vinegar, olive oil, salt, and pepper in a small bowl. 6. In a salad bowl, combine the rocket with the cooled figs and chickpeas. 7. Drizzle the dressing over the salad, toss to combine, and serve.

Crispy Honey Cinnamon Sweet Potato Bites

Prep time: 10 minutes | Cook time: 25 minutes | Serves 4

- Oil, for spraying
- 3 medium sweet potatoes, peeled and cut into 1-inch pieces
- 2 tablespoons honey
- 1 tablespoon olive oil
- 2 teaspoons ground cinnamon

1. Line the air fryer basket with parchment and spray lightly with oil. 2. In a large bowl, toss together the sweet potatoes, honey, olive oil, and cinnamon until evenly coated. 3. Place the potatoes in the prepared basket. 4. Air fry at 200°C for 20 to 25 minutes, or until crispy and easily pierced with a fork.

Portobello Pepperoni Marinara Pizzas

Prep time: 5 minutes | Cook time: 18 minutes | Serves 4

- 4 large portobello mushrooms, stems removed
- 4 teaspoons olive oil
- 225 g marinara sauce
- 225 g shredded Mozzarella cheese
- 10 slices sugar-free pepperoni

1. Preheat the air fryer to 190°C. 2. Brush each mushroom cap with the olive oil, one teaspoon for each cap. 3. Put on a baking sheet and bake, stem-side down, for 8 minutes. 4. Take out of the air fryer and divide the marinara sauce, Mozzarella cheese and pepperoni evenly among the caps. 5. Air fry for another 10 minutes until browned. 6. Serve hot.

Buttery Mushrooms

Prep time: 10 minutes | Cook time: 10 minutes | Serves 4

- 230 g shitake mushrooms, halved
- 2 tablespoons salted butter, melted
- ¼ teaspoon salt
- ¼ teaspoon ground black pepper

1. Begin by placing the mushrooms in a medium bowl and tossing them with melted butter. Season with salt and pepper, making sure they are well-coated. 2. Transfer the seasoned mushrooms to the ungreased air fryer basket, spreading them out evenly. 3. Set the air fryer temperature to 200°C and air fry for 10 minutes, shaking the basket halfway through to ensure even cooking. The mushrooms will be tender and golden when done. 4. Serve the mushrooms warm, enjoying their rich, buttery flavor.

Caramelized Aubergine with Spicy Harissa Yogurt

Prep time: 10 minutes | Cook time: 15 minutes | Serves 2

- 1 medium aubergine (about 340 g), cut crosswise into ½-inch-thick slices and quartered
- 2 tablespoons vegetable oil
- coarse sea salt and freshly ground black pepper, to taste
- 120 g plain yoghurt (not Greek)
- 2 tablespoons harissa paste
- 1 garlic clove, grated
- 2 teaspoons honey

1. In a bowl, toss together the aubergine and oil, season with salt and pepper, and toss to coat evenly. Transfer to the air fryer and air fry at 200°C, shaking the basket every 5 minutes, until the aubergine is caramelized and tender, about 15 minutes. 2. Meanwhile, in a small bowl, whisk together the yoghurt, harissa, and garlic, then spread onto a serving plate. 3. Pile the warm aubergine over the yoghurt and drizzle with the honey just before serving.

Mexican Maize in a Cup

Prep time: 5 minutes | Cook time: 10 minutes | Serves 4

- 650 g frozen maize kernels (do not thaw)
- Vegetable oil spray
- 2 tablespoons butter
- 60 g sour cream
- 60 g mayonnaise
- 20 g grated Parmesan cheese (or feta, cotija, or queso fresco)
- 2 tablespoons fresh lemon or lime juice
- 1 teaspoon chilli powder
- Chopped fresh green onion (optional)
- Chopped fresh coriander (optional)

1. Begin by placing the maize in the bottom of the air fryer basket and lightly spraying it with vegetable oil spray. Set the air fryer to 180°C and cook for 10 minutes. 2. Once done, transfer the maize to a serving bowl. Add the butter and stir until it melts completely. Then, add the sour cream, mayonnaise, cheese, lemon juice, and chili powder, stirring everything together until smooth and well combined. 3. Serve immediately, topped with green onion and coriander if desired, for an extra burst of flavor.

Bread Rolls

Prep time: 10 minutes | Cook time: 12 minutes | Serves 6

- 225 g shredded Mozzarella cheese
- 30 g full-fat cream cheese
- 95 g blanched finely ground almond flour
- 40 g ground flaxseed
- ½ teaspoon baking powder
- 1 large egg

1. In a large microwave-safe bowl, combine mozzarella, cream cheese, and almond flour. Microwave the mixture for 1 minute, then stir until smooth and well combined. 2. Add the flaxseed, baking powder, and egg to the mixture, stirring until everything is fully incorporated and smooth. If the dough becomes too firm, microwave it for an additional 15 seconds. 3. Divide the dough into six equal portions and shape each into a ball. Place the dough balls in the air fryer basket. 4. Set the air fryer to 160°C and cook the rolls for 12 minutes, or until golden and cooked through. 5. Once done, let the rolls cool completely before serving to maintain their texture.

Garlicky Baked Cherry Tomatoes

Prep time: 5 minutes | Cook time: 4 to 6 minutes | Serves 2

- 475 g cherry tomatoes
- 1 clove garlic, thinly sliced
- 1 teaspoon olive oil
- ⅛ teaspoon rock salt
- 1 tablespoon freshly chopped basil, for topping
- Cooking spray

1. Start by preheating the air fryer to 180°C. 2. Lightly coat the air fryer baking dish with cooking spray to prevent sticking, then set it aside. 3. In a large bowl, combine the cherry tomatoes, thinly sliced garlic, olive oil, and a sprinkle of rock salt. Toss until everything is evenly coated. 4. Spread the tomato mixture evenly in the prepared baking dish. 5. Place the dish in the preheated air fryer and cook for 4 to 6 minutes, or until the tomatoes soften and start to wilt. 6. After cooking, transfer the tomatoes to a bowl and allow them to rest for 5 minutes, letting the flavors settle. 7. Top with freshly chopped basil and serve while warm for a burst of fresh flavor.

Garlic Parmesan-Roasted Cauliflower

Prep time: 5 minutes | Cook time: 15 minutes | Serves 6

- 1 medium head cauliflower, leaves and core removed, cut into florets
- 2 tablespoons salted butter, melted
- ½ tablespoon salt
- 2 cloves garlic, peeled and finely minced
- 45 g grated Parmesan cheese, divided

1. In a large bowl, toss the cauliflower florets with melted butter. Season with salt, garlic, and half of the Parmesan cheese, ensuring the florets are well coated. 2. Place the cauliflower florets into the ungreased air fryer basket. Set the air fryer to 180°C and cook for 15 minutes, shaking the basket halfway through to ensure even roasting. The cauliflower will be tender with browned edges when done. 3. Once cooked, transfer the florets to a large serving dish and sprinkle with the remaining Parmesan cheese. Serve warm for the best flavor.

Chapter 9

Vegetarian Mains

Chapter 9 Vegetarian Mains

Cheesy Cabbage Wedges

Prep time: 5 minutes | Cook time: 20 minutes | Serves 4

- 4 tablespoons melted butter
- 1 head cabbage, cut into wedges
- 235 g shredded Parmesan cheese
- Salt and black pepper, to taste
- 120 g shredded Mozzarella cheese

1. Start by preheating the air fryer to 190°C. 2. Brush the melted butter generously over the cut sides of the cabbage wedges. Sprinkle both sides evenly with Parmesan cheese. 3. Season the wedges with salt and pepper to taste, ensuring all surfaces are well-seasoned. 4. Place the cabbage wedges into the air fryer basket and cook for 20 minutes, flipping them halfway through the cooking time, until the edges are lightly browned and the cabbage is tender. 5. Once done, transfer the cabbage wedges to a plate and sprinkle with Mozzarella cheese before serving.

Savory Mushroom and Barley Pilaf

Prep time: 5 minutes | Cook time: 37 minutes | Serves 4

- Olive oil cooking spray
- 2 tablespoons olive oil
- 227 g button mushrooms, diced
- ½ brown onion, diced
- 2 garlic cloves, minced
- 235 ml pearl barley
- 475 ml vegetable broth
- 1 tablespoon fresh thyme, chopped
- ½ teaspoon salt
- ¼ teaspoon smoked paprika
- Fresh parsley, for garnish

1. Preheat the air fryer to 192°C. 2. Lightly coat the inside of a 1.2 L capacity casserole dish with olive oil cooking spray. (The shape of the casserole dish will depend upon the size of the air fryer, but it needs to be able to hold at least 1.2 L.) 3. In a large skillet, heat the olive oil over medium heat. 4. Add the mushrooms and onion and cook, stirring occasionally, for 5 minutes, or until the mushrooms begin to brown. 5. Add the garlic and cook for an additional 2 minutes. 6. Transfer the vegetables to a large bowl. 7. Add the barley, broth, thyme, salt, and paprika. 8. Pour the barley-and-vegetable mixture into the prepared casserole dish and place the dish into the air fryer. 9. Bake for 15 minutes. 10. Stir the barley mixture. Reduce the heat to 182°C, then return the barley to the air fryer and bake for 15 minutes more. 11.Remove from the air fryer and let sit for 5 minutes before fluffing with a fork and topping with fresh parsley.

Moroccan-Inspired Chickpea and Rice Bake

Prep time: 10 minutes | Cook time: 45 minutes | Serves 6

- Olive oil cooking spray
- 235 ml long-grain brown rice
- 535 ml chicken stock
- 1 (439 g) can chickpeas, drained and rinsed
- 120 ml diced carrot
- 120 ml green peas
- 1 teaspoon ground cumin
- ½ teaspoon ground turmeric
- ½ teaspoon ground ginger
- ½ teaspoon onion powder
- ½ teaspoon salt
- ¼ teaspoon ground cinnamon
- ¼ teaspoon garlic powder
- ¼ teaspoon black pepper
- Fresh parsley, for garnish

1. Preheat the air fryer to 192°C. 2. Lightly coat the inside of a 1.2 L capacity casserole dish with olive oil cooking spray. (The shape of the casserole dish will depend upon the size of the air fryer, but it needs to be able to hold at least 1.2 L.) 3. In the casserole dish, combine the rice, stock, chickpeas, carrot, peas, cumin, turmeric, ginger, onion powder, salt, cinnamon, garlic powder, and black pepper. 4. Stir well to combine. 5. Cover loosely with aluminium foil. 6. Place the covered casserole dish into the air fryer and bake for 20 minutes. 7. Remove from the air fryer and stir well. 8. Place the casserole back into the air fryer, uncovered, and bake for 25 minutes more. 9. Fluff with a spoon and sprinkle with fresh chopped parsley before serving.

Sweet Potato Black Bean Burgers

Prep time: 10 minutes | Cook time: 10 minutes | Serves 4

- 1 (425 g) can black beans, drained and rinsed
- 235 ml mashed sweet potato
- ½ teaspoon dried oregano
- ¼ teaspoon dried thyme
- ¼ teaspoon dried marjoram
- 1 garlic clove, minced
- ¼ teaspoon salt
- ¼ teaspoon black pepper
- 1 tablespoon lemon juice
- 235 ml cooked brown rice
- 60 to 120 ml wholemeal breadcrumbs
- 1 tablespoon olive oil

For serving:
- Wholemeal buns or wholemeal pittas
- Plain Greek yoghurt
- Avocado
- Lettuce
- Tomato
- Red onion

1. Preheat the air fryer to 192°C. 2. In a large bowl, mash the black beans with the back of a fork until smooth, with no large chunks remaining. 3. Add the mashed sweet potato, oregano, thyme, marjoram, garlic, salt, pepper, and lemon juice to the beans, stirring until everything is well combined. 4. Mix in the cooked rice, ensuring it's evenly distributed throughout the mixture. 5. Gradually add 60 ml of wholemeal breadcrumbs and stir until the mixture thickens. 6. If the mixture is too wet to form patties, add another 60 ml of breadcrumbs and mix well until it reaches the right consistency. 7. Shape the mixture into 4 evenly sized patties. 8. Arrange the patties in the air fryer basket in a single layer, ensuring they don't touch each other. 9. Brush half of the olive oil over the patties and air fry for 5 minutes. 10. Flip the patties over, brush the remaining olive oil on the other side, and air fry for another 4 to 5 minutes until golden and crispy. 11. Serve the patties on toasted wholemeal buns or pittas, topped with a spoonful of yogurt, avocado, lettuce, tomato, and red onion for a delicious, hearty meal.

Cheesy Spinach Egg Pie

Prep time: 10 minutes | Cook time: 20 minutes | Serves 4

- 6 large eggs
- 60 ml double cream
- 235 g frozen chopped spinach, drained
- 235 g shredded sharp Cheddar cheese
- 60 g diced brown onion

1. In a medium bowl, whisk eggs and add cream. Add remaining ingredients to bowl. Pour into a round baking dish. Place into the air fryer basket. Adjust the temperature to 160°C and bake for 20 minutes. 2.Eggs will be firm and slightly browned when cooked. 3.Serve immediately.

Aubergine Parmesan

Prep time: 15 minutes | Cook time: 17 minutes | Serves 4

- 1 medium aubergine, ends trimmed, sliced into ½-inch rounds
- ¼ teaspoon salt
- 2 tablespoons coconut oil
- 120 g grated Parmesan cheese
- 30 g cheese crisps, finely crushed
- 120 ml low-carb marinara sauce
- 120 g shredded Mozzarella cheese

1. Start by sprinkling the aubergine rounds with salt on both sides and wrap them in a kitchen towel. Let them sit for 30 minutes to allow excess moisture to be drawn out. 2. After 30 minutes, press the rounds gently to remove any remaining water, then drizzle both sides with coconut oil. 3. In a medium bowl, combine Parmesan cheese with cheese crisps. 4. Dip each aubergine slice into the cheese mixture, pressing lightly to coat both sides thoroughly. 5. Place the coated aubergine rounds into the ungreased air fryer basket. 6. Set the air fryer to 180°C and cook for 15 minutes, flipping the rounds halfway through, until they are crispy around the edges. 7. Once crispy, spoon marinara sauce over the aubergine rounds and top with Mozzarella cheese. 8. Continue cooking for an additional 2 minutes at 180°C, or until the cheese has melted. 9. Serve the cheesy aubergine rounds warm and enjoy!

Cheesy Sweet Pepper Nachos

Prep time: 10 minutes | Cook time: 5 minutes | Serves 2

- 6 mini sweet peppers, seeded and sliced in half
- 180 g shredded Colby jack or Monterey Jack cheese
- 60 g sliced pickled jalapeños
- ½ medium avocado, peeled, pitted, and diced
- 2 tablespoons sour cream

1. Place peppers into an ungreased round non-stick baking dish. 2.Sprinkle with cheese and top with jalapeños. 3.Place dish into air fryer basket. 4.Adjust the temperature to 180°C and bake for 5 minutes. 5.Cheese will be melted and bubbly when done. 6.Remove dish from air fryer and top with avocado. 7.Drizzle with sour cream. 8.Serve warm.

Teriyaki Cauliflower

Prep time: 5 minutes | Cook time: 14 minutes | Serves 4

- 120 ml soy sauce
- 80 ml water
- 1 tablespoon brown sugar
- 1 teaspoon sesame oil
- 1 teaspoon cornflour
- 2 cloves garlic, chopped
- ½ teaspoon chilli powder
- 1 big cauliflower head, cut into florets

1. Begin by preheating the air fryer to 170°C. 2. Prepare the teriyaki sauce by whisking together soy sauce, water, brown sugar, sesame oil, cornflour, garlic, and chili powder in a small bowl until smooth and well combined. 3. Place the cauliflower florets in a large bowl, then drizzle the teriyaki sauce over the top. Toss the florets thoroughly to coat them evenly with the sauce. 4. Transfer the coated cauliflower florets to the air fryer basket and air fry for 14 minutes, shaking the basket halfway through, until the cauliflower is crisp on the outside and tender on the inside. 5. Once cooked, let the cauliflower rest for 5 minutes before serving to allow the flavors to set.

Mediterranean Air Fried Veggies

Prep time: 10 minutes | Cook time: 6 minutes | Serves 4

- 1 large courgette, sliced
- 235 g cherry tomatoes, halved
- 1 parsnip, sliced
- 1 green pepper, sliced
- 1 carrot, sliced
- 1 teaspoon mixed herbs
- 1 teaspoon mustard
- 1 teaspoon garlic purée
- 6 tablespoons olive oil
- Salt and ground black pepper, to taste

1. Preheat the air fryer to 200°C. 2. In a large bowl, combine all the ingredients, tossing the vegetables well to ensure they are evenly coated. 3. Transfer the seasoned vegetables to the air fryer basket and air fry for 6 minutes, checking that they are tender and lightly browned. 4. Once done, serve immediately for the best flavor and texture.

Greek-Style Baked Beans with Feta

Prep time: 5 minutes | Cook time: 30 minutes | Serves 4

- Olive oil cooking spray
- 1 (425 g) can cannellini beans, drained and rinsed
- 1 (425 g) can butter beans, drained and rinsed
- ½ brown onion, diced
- 1 (230 g) can tomato sauce
- 1½ tablespoons raw honey
- 60 ml olive oil
- 2 garlic cloves, minced
- 2 tablespoons chopped fresh dill
- ½ teaspoon salt
- ½ teaspoon black pepper
- 1 bay leaf
- 1 tablespoon balsamic vinegar
- 60 g feta cheese, crumbled, for serving

1. Preheat the air fryer to 182°C. 2. Lightly coat the inside of a 1.2 L capacity casserole dish with olive oil cooking spray. (The shape of the casserole dish will depend upon the size of the air fryer, but it needs to be able to hold at least 1.2 L.) 3. In a large bowl, combine all ingredients except the feta cheese and stir until well combined. 4. Pour the bean mixture into the prepared casserole dish. 5. Bake in the air fryer for 30 minutes. 6. Remove from the air fryer and remove and discard the bay leaf. 7. Sprinkle crumbled feta over the top before serving.

Chapter 10

Desserts

Chapter 10 Desserts

Cream-Filled Air-Fried Sponge Cakes

Prep time: 10 minutes | Cook time: 10 minutes | Makes 4 cakes

- Coconut, or avocado oil, for spraying
- 1 tube croissant dough
- 4 Swiss rolls
- 1 tablespoon icing sugar

1. Line the air fryer basket with baking paper, and spray lightly with oil. 2. Unroll the dough into a single flat layer and cut it into 4 equal pieces. 3. Place 1 sponge cake in the center of each piece of dough. Wrap the dough around the cake, pinching the ends to seal. 4. Place the wrapped cakes in the prepared basket, and spray lightly with oil. 5. Bake at 90°C for 5 minutes, flip, spray with oil, and cook for another 5 minutes, or until golden brown. 6. Dust with the icing sugar and serve.

Carrot Cake with Cream Cheese Icing

Prep time: 10 minutes | Cook time: 55 minutes | Serves 6 to 8

- 80 g Plain flour
- 1 teaspoon baking powder
- ½ teaspoon baking soda
- 1 teaspoon ground cinnamon
- ¼ teaspoon ground nutmeg
- ¼ teaspoon salt

Icing:
- 225 g cream cheese, softened at room temperature
- 8 tablespoons butter, softened at room
- 3 to 4 medium carrots or 2 large, grated
- 120 g granulated sugar
- 35 g brown sugar
- 2 eggs
- 175 ml canola or vegetable oil

temperature
- 70 g icing sugar
- 1 teaspoon pure vanilla extract

1. Grease a cake pan with butter or oil to prevent sticking. 2. In a mixing bowl, combine flour, baking powder, baking soda, cinnamon, nutmeg, and salt. Add the grated carrots and toss them well to coat. In a separate bowl, beat together the sugars and eggs until light and frothy. Slowly drizzle in the oil while continuing to beat the mixture. Gently fold the egg mixture into the dry ingredients until everything is just combined and no flour is visible. Pour the batter into the greased cake pan and wrap the pan tightly in greased aluminum foil. 3. Preheat the air fryer to 180°C. 4. Using a sling made from aluminum foil (fold a strip about 2 inches wide and 24 inches long), carefully lower the cake pan into the air fryer basket. Fold the foil ends over the top of the cake to cover it. Air fry for 40 minutes. Afterward, remove the foil cover and air fry for an additional 15 minutes or until a skewer inserted into the center comes out clean, and the top is golden brown. 5. While the cake is baking, prepare the cream cheese frosting by beating together cream cheese, butter, icing sugar, and vanilla extract with a hand mixer, stand mixer, or food processor until smooth and fluffy. 6. Once the cake is done, allow it to cool in the pan for about 10 minutes. Then remove the cake from the pan and let it cool completely on a wire rack. Frost the cooled cake with the cream cheese icing and serve.

Baked Apples and Walnuts

Prep time: 6 minutes | Cook time: 20 minutes | Serves 4

- 4 small Granny Smith apples
- 50 g chopped walnuts
- 40 g light brown sugar
- 2 tablespoons butter, melted
- 1 teaspoon ground cinnamon
- ½ teaspoon ground nutmeg
- 120 ml water, or apple juice

1. Start by cutting off the top third of the apples and carefully spooning out the core and some of the flesh. Discard the core and extra flesh. Place the hollowed-out apples into a small air fryer baking pan. 2. Insert the crisper plate into the basket and then place the basket into the air fryer unit. Preheat the air fryer to 180°C. 3. In a small bowl, mix the walnuts, brown sugar, melted butter, cinnamon, and nutmeg until well combined. Spoon this mixture into the hollow centers of the apples, packing it in gently. 4. Once the air fryer is preheated, pour a small amount of water into the crisper plate to help steam the apples. Place the baking pan with the stuffed apples into the basket. 5. Air fry the apples for 20 minutes. 6. When the cooking time is complete, the apples should be soft, bubbly, and fork-tender, ready to serve.

Strawberry Pastry Rolls

Prep time: 20 minutes | Cook time: 5 to 6 minutes per batch | Serves 4

- 85 g low-fat cream cheese
- 2 tablespoons plain yoghurt
- 2 teaspoons granulated sugar
- ¼ teaspoon pure vanilla extract
- 225 g fresh strawberries
- 8 sheets filo pastry
- Butter-flavoured cooking spray
- 45-90 g dark chocolate crisps (optional)

1. In a medium bowl, combine cream cheese, yogurt, sugar, and vanilla. Use a hand mixer on high speed to beat until smooth, about 1 minute. 2. Wash and destem the strawberries. Chop enough to measure 80 g, then stir them into the cheese mixture. 3. Preheat the air fryer to 160ºC. 4. Since filo pastry dries out quickly, cover your stack of sheets with baking paper and then place a damp dish towel on top. Only remove one sheet at a time while you work. 5. To create one pastry roll, lay a single sheet of filo on a flat surface. Lightly spray it with butter-flavored spray, then place a second sheet on top and spray it as well. 6. Spoon about 3 tablespoons of the cheese mixture (a quarter of the filling) about ½ inch from the edge of one short side. Fold the edge of the filo over the filling, then continue rolling it a turn or two. Fold in both the left and right sides to seal the roll, and then continue rolling until fully wrapped. Spray the outside of the roll with butter spray. 7. Repeat the process to make 4 rolls and place them seam side down in the air fryer basket, leaving space between each. Air fry for 5 to 6 minutes, or until they turn golden brown. 8. Repeat step 7 with the remaining rolls. 9. Allow the pastries to cool to room temperature. 10. When ready to serve, slice the remaining strawberries. If desired, melt chocolate crisps using a microwave or double boiler. Place one pastry on each dessert plate, top with sliced strawberries, and drizzle melted chocolate over the strawberries and onto the plate for an extra indulgence.

New York Cheesecake

Prep time: 1 hour | Cook time: 37 minutes | Serves 8

- 65 g almond flour
- 45 g powdered sweetener
- 55 g unsalted butter, melted
- 565 g full-fat cream cheese
- 120 ml double cream
- 340 g granulated sweetener
- 3 eggs, at room temperature
- 1 tablespoon vanilla essence
- 1 teaspoon grated lemon zest

1. Lightly coat the sides and bottom of a baking pan with flour to prevent sticking. 2. In a mixing bowl, combine almond flour and powdered sweetener. Add the melted butter and mix until the texture resembles breadcrumbs. 3. Press this mixture firmly into the bottom of the prepared pan, creating an even layer. Bake at 160ºC for 7 minutes, or until the crust is golden brown. Let it cool completely on a wire rack. 4. In the meantime, prepare the filling by mixing soft cheese, double cream, and granulated sweetener in a stand mixer with the paddle attachment. Beat until the mixture is creamy and fluffy. 5. Add the eggs one at a time, followed by the vanilla extract and lemon zest. Continue mixing until everything is well combined. 6. Pour the cheesecake filling over the cooled crust, spreading it evenly with a spatula. 7. Bake in the preheated air fryer at 160ºC for 25 to 30 minutes. After baking, leave the cheesecake in the air fryer to keep warm for another 30 minutes. 8. Cover the cheesecake with cling film and refrigerate for at least 6 hours or overnight to set. Serve well chilled.

Orange, Anise & Ginger Skillet Cookie with Icing

Prep time: 20 minutes | Cook time: 15 minutes | Serves 2 to 4

Cookie:
- Vegetable oil
- 65 g Plain flour, plus 2 tablespoons
- 1 tablespoon grated orange zest
- 1 teaspoon ground ginger
- 1 teaspoon aniseeds, crushed
- ¼ teaspoon kosher, or coarse sea salt
- 4 tablespoons unsalted butter, at room temperature
- 80 g granulated sugar, plus more for sprinkling
- 3 tablespoons black treacle
- 1 large egg

Icing:
- 30 g icing sugar
- 2 to 3 teaspoons milk

1. For the cookie: Generously grease a baking pan with vegetable oil. 2. In a medium bowl, whisk together the flour, orange zest, ginger, aniseeds, and salt. 3. In a medium bowl using a hand mixer, beat the butter and sugar on medium-high speed until well combined, about 2 minutes. Add the treacle and egg and beat until light in color, about 2 minutes. Add the flour mixture and mix on low until just combined. Use a rubber spatula to scrape the dough into the prepared pan, spreading it to the edges and smoothing the top. Sprinkle with sugar. 4. Place the pan in the basket. Set the air fryer to 160ºC and bake for 15 minutes, or until sides are browned but the center is still quite soft. 5. Let cool in the pan on a wire rack for 15 minutes. Turn the biscuit out of the pan onto the rack. 6. For the icing: Whisk together the sugar and 2 teaspoons of milk. Add 1 teaspoon milk if needed for the desired consistency. Spread, or drizzle onto the cookie.

Crispy Air Fryer Apple Fritters

Prep time: 30 minutes | Cook time: 7 to 8 minutes | Serves 6

- 1 chopped, peeled Granny Smith apple
- 90 g granulated sugar
- 1 teaspoon ground cinnamon
- 60 g Plain flour
- 1 teaspoon baking powder
- 1 teaspoon salt
- 2 tablespoons milk
- 2 tablespoons butter, melted
- 1 large egg, beaten
- Cooking spray
- 15 g icing sugar (optional)

1. Mix together the apple, granulated sugar, and cinnamon in a small bowl. Allow to sit for 30 minutes. 2. Combine the flour, baking powder, and salt in a medium bowl. Add the milk, butter, and egg and stir to incorporate. 3. Pour the apple mixture into the bowl of flour mixture and stir with a spatula until a dough forms. 4. Make the fritters: On a clean work surface, divide the dough into 12 equal portions and shape into 1-inch balls. Flatten them into patties with your hands. 5. Preheat the air fryer to 180°C. Line the air fryer basket with baking paper and spray it with cooking spray. 6. Transfer the apple fritters onto the baking paper, evenly spaced but not too close together. Spray the fritters with cooking spray. 7. Bake for 7 to 8 minutes until lightly browned. Flip the fritters halfway through the cooking time. 8. Remove from the basket to a plate and serve with the confectioners' sugar sprinkled on top, if desired.

Gluten-Free Spice Cookies

Prep time: 10 minutes | Cook time: 12 minutes | Serves 4

- 4 tablespoons unsalted butter, at room temperature
- 2 tablespoons agave nectar
- 1 large egg
- 2 tablespoons water
- 120 g almond flour
- 80 g granulated sugar
- 2 teaspoons ground ginger
- 1 teaspoon ground cinnamon
- ½ teaspoon freshly grated nutmeg
- 1 teaspoon baking soda
- ¼ teaspoon kosher, or coarse sea salt

1. Start by lining the bottom of the air fryer basket with a piece of baking paper cut to fit. 2. In a large bowl, use a hand mixer to beat the butter, agave, egg, and water on medium speed until the mixture becomes light and fluffy. 3. Add the almond flour, sugar, ginger, cinnamon, nutmeg, baking soda, and salt to the bowl. Beat on low speed until everything is fully combined. 4. Roll the dough into 2-tablespoon-sized balls and place them on the baking paper in the air fryer basket, leaving a little space between each one (they don't spread much during cooking). Set the air fryer to 160°C and cook for 12 minutes, or until the tops of the cookies are lightly browned. 5. Once cooked, transfer the cookies to a wire rack and allow them to cool completely. Store in an airtight container for up to a week.

Air-Fried Gingerbread Loaf

Prep time: 5 minutes | Cook time: 20 minutes | Makes 1 loaf

- Cooking spray
- 65 g Plain flour
- 2 tablespoons granulated sugar
- ¾ teaspoon ground ginger
- ¼ teaspoon cinnamon
- 1 teaspoon baking powder
- ½ teaspoon baking soda
- ⅛ teaspoon salt
- 1 egg
- 70 g treacle
- 120 ml buttermilk
- 2 tablespoons coconut, or avocado oil
- 1 teaspoon pure vanilla extract

1. Preheat the air fryer to 160°C. 2. Spray a baking dish lightly with cooking spray. 3. In a medium bowl, mix together all the dry ingredients. 4. In a separate bowl, beat the egg. Add treacle, buttermilk, oil, and vanilla and stir until well mixed. 5. Pour liquid mixture into dry ingredients and stir until well blended. 6. Pour batter into baking dish and bake for 20 minutes, or until toothpick inserted in center of loaf comes out clean.

Low-Carb Vanilla Pound Cake

Prep time: 10 minutes | Cook time: 25 minutes | Serves 6

- 55 g blanched finely ground almond flour
- 55 g salted butter, melted
- 100 g granulated sweetener
- 1 teaspoon vanilla extract
- 1 teaspoon baking powder
- 120 ml full-fat sour cream
- 30 g full-fat cream cheese, softened
- 2 large eggs

1. In a large bowl, mix almond flour, butter, and sweetener. 2. Add in vanilla, baking powder, sour cream, and cream cheese and mix until well combined. Add eggs and mix. 3. Pour batter into round baking pan. Place pan into the air fryer basket. 4. Adjust the temperature to 150°C and bake for 25 minutes. 5. When the cake is done, a toothpick inserted in center will come out clean. The center should not feel wet. Allow it to cool completely, or the cake will crumble when moved.

Appendix 1: Basic Kitchen Conversions & Equivalents

DRY MEASUREMENTS CONVERSION CHART

3 teaspoons = 1 tablespoon = 1/16 cup

6 teaspoons = 2 tablespoons = 1/8 cup

12 teaspoons = 4 tablespoons = 1/4 cup

24 teaspoons = 8 tablespoons = 1/2 cup

36 teaspoons = 12 tablespoons = 3/4 cup

48 teaspoons = 16 tablespoons = 1 cup

METRIC TO US COOKING CONVERSIONS

OVEN TEMPERATURES

120 °C = 250 °F

160 °C = 320 °F

180 °C = 350 °F

205 °C = 400 °F

220 °C = 425 °F

LIQUID MEASUREMENTS CONVERSION CHART

8 fluid ounces = 1 cup = 1/2 pint = 1/4 quart

16 fluid ounces = 2 cups = 1 pint = 1/2 quart

32 fluid ounces = 4 cups = 2 pints = 1 quart = 1/4 gallon

128 fluid ounces = 16 cups = 8 pints = 4 quarts = 1 gallon

BAKING IN GRAMS

1 cup flour = 140 grams

1 cup sugar = 150 grams

1 cup powdered sugar = 160 grams

1 cup heavy cream = 235 grams

VOLUME

1 milliliter = 1/5 tsp

5 ml = 1 tsp

15 ml = 1 tbsp

240 ml = 1 cup or 8 fluid ounces

1 liter = 34 fluid ounces

WEIGHT

1 gram = 0.035 ounces

100 grams = 3.5 ounces

500 grams = 1.1 pounds

1 kilogram = 35 ounces

Appendix 2: Recipes Index

A

Air Fried Beef Satay with Peanut Dipping Sauce	45
Air-Fried Gingerbread Loaf	72
Air-Fried Sirloin with Honey-Mustard Butter	48
Airy Delight Toaster Treats	10
Almond Bliss Pancakes	9
Aubergine Parmesan	67

B

Bacon & Egg Breakfast Cups	9
Bacon and Cheese Stuffed Pork Chops	47
Bacon, Egg, and Cheese Roll Ups	8
Bacon-and-Eggs Avocado	11
Bacon-Wrapped Hot Dogs	14
Bacon-Wrapped Meat Roll	42
Bacon-Wrapped Pork Tenderloin	43
Baked Apples and Walnuts	70
Baked Cheese Sandwich	19
Baked Peach Porridge	12
Balsamic Steak & Veggie Skewers	14
Banger and Peppers	45
Basil Lentil-Stuffed Tomatoes with Goat Cheese	19
Beef and Mango Skewers	53
Beef Burger	44
Beery and Crunchy Onion Rings	20
Beetroot Salad with Lemon Vinaigrette	18
Berry Bliss Breakfast Tarts	6
Blackened Steak Nuggets	42
Blueberry Cobbler	11
Bread Rolls	64
Breakfast Banger and Cauliflower	12
Butter and Bacon Chicken	24
Buttery Mushrooms	63
Buttery Sweet Potatoes	19

C

Cajun Bacon-Wrapped Pork Loin Fillet	43
Cajun Shrimp & Veggie Skillet	14
Caramelized Aubergine with Spicy Harissa Yogurt	63
Carrot Cake with Cream Cheese Icing	70
Cheesy Cabbage Wedges	66
Cheesy Chilli Toast	18
Cheesy Crescent Dogs	46
Cheesy Spinach Delight Omelet	7
Cheesy Spinach Egg Pie	67
Cheesy Sweet Pepper Nachos	67
Chicken Burgers with Gammon and Cheese	27
Chicken Schnitzel Hot Dogs	27
Chicken Wings with Piri Piri Sauce	30
Chicken with Lettuce	28
Chilean Sea Bass with Zesty Olive Relish	39
Chilli-brined Fried Calamari	56
Classic Air-Fried Scotch Eggs	55
Classic Spring Rolls	56
Classic Whole Chicken	23
Coconut Prawns with Pineapple-Lemon Sauce	38
Courgette Fritters	60
Cream-Filled Air-Fried Sponge Cakes	70
Creamy Fish Gratin with Swiss Cheese Topping	34
Creamy Greek Yogurt Deviled Eggs	53
Crispy Air Fryer Apple Fritters	72
Crispy Air-Fried Chicken-Fried Steak with Gravy	46
Crispy Air-Fried Mozzarella Arancini	53
Crispy Almond-Crusted Lemon Fish	37
Crispy Bacon-Wrapped Scallops	33
Crispy Brussels Sprouts with Toasted Pecans and Gorgonzola	62
Crispy Chorizo Scotch Eggs	19
Crispy Coconut Prawns with Spicy Lime Sauce	35
Crispy Duck with Cherry Sauce	29
Crispy Filo Artichoke Triangles	54
Crispy Golden Chicken Tenders	25
Crispy Herb Breaded Turkey Cutlets	28
Crispy Herbed Lentil Rice Bites	52
Crispy Homemade Croutons	20
Crispy Honey Cinnamon Sweet Potato Bites	63
Crispy Lemony Pear Chips	52
Crispy Lemony Roasted Broccoli	60
Crispy Lime-Spiced Chicken Thighs	28
Crispy Parmesan-Coated Chicken Breasts	22
Crispy Parmesan-Crusted Lobster Tails	34
Crispy Prawn Egg Rolls	57
Crispy Roasted Potatoes with Asparagus Mash	61

Crispy String Bean Fries	57
Crispy Sweet Potato Fries with Spicy Mayo Dip	54
Crispy Tuna Avocado Bites	38
Crispy Tuna Patties with Beer Cheese Sauce	40
Crunchy Basil White Beans	52
Crunchy Dill-Coated Chicken Strips	26
Curry-Spiced Cranberry Chicken Bowls	24

E

Easy Banger Pizza	8

F

Fiesta Lime Chicken Bowl	24
Fig, Chickpea, and Rocket Salad	62
Five-Ingredient Falafel with Garlic-Yoghurt Sauce	57
Fried Green Tomatoes	15

G

Garlic Basil Prawn Pasta with Mushrooms	32
Garlic Herb Roasted Vegetables	20
Garlic Parmesan-Roasted Cauliflower	64
Garlic Prawns	40
Garlic Rosemary Ribeye Steaks	42
Garlic Soy Chicken Thighs	30
Garlicky Baked Cherry Tomatoes	64
Garlic-Thyme Roasted Tomatoes	61
Glazed Piri-Piri Chicken Thighs	29
Gluten-Free Spice Cookies	72
Golden Air-Fried Crab Cakes	33
Golden Banana Walnut Loaf	6
Golden Banana Walnut Muffins	7
Golden Beer-Battered Cod	32
Golden Berry Crumble Delight	14
Golden Cheesy Potato Patties	18
Golden Crispy Air-Fried Latkes	53
Golden Melt Breakfast Quesadillas	10
Gourmet Cauliflower Crust Pizzas	16
Greek-Style Baked Beans with Feta	68
Greek-Style Herb-Infused Meatloaf	47
Greens Crisps with Curried Yoghurt Sauce	54

H

Healthy Veggie Salmon Nachos	54
Herbed Sunrise Pitta	8
Herbed Turkey Apple Patties	10
Hoisin Turkey Burgers	28
Honey-Sesame Carrots and Sugar Snap Peas	62

I

Italian Egg Cups	6
Italian Pork Loin	44

J

Juicy Air-Fried Turkey Tenderloin	24

K

Kale Salad Sushi Rolls with Sriracha Mayonnaise	55
Kheema Meatloaf	44

L

Lamb Chops with Horseradish Sauce	47
Lemon Chicken with Garlic	26
Lemon Thyme Roasted Chicken	30
Lemon-Blueberry Muffins	7
Lemon-Tarragon Fish en Papillote	33
Lemony Curried Endive with Yogurt Marinade	56
Low-Carb Vanilla Pound Cake	72

M

Macadamia-Crusted Pork Rack	43
Maple-Roasted Tomatoes	61
Meatball Subs	16
Mediterranean Air Fried Veggies	68
Mexican Maize in a Cup	63
Mixed Berry Bliss Muffins	8
Moroccan-Inspired Chickpea and Rice Bake	66
Mushroom in Bacon-Wrapped Filets Mignons	43

N

Nashville Hot Chicken	25
New York Cheesecake	71

O

Onion Omelette	9

Orange, Anise & Ginger Skillet Cookie with Icing	71
Oyster Po'Boy	36

P

Parmesan-Crusted Italian Chicken with Mozzarella Sauce	23
Parmesan-Rosemary Radishes	61
Peanut Butter Chicken Satay	22
Pecan Rolls	15
Peppercorn-Crusted Beef Fillet	46
Pork Loin with Aloha Salsa	50
Pork Rind Fried Chicken	29
Portobello Pepperoni Marinara Pizzas	63
Prawn Bake	38
Prawns Scampi	36
Prawns with Smoky Tomato Dressing	37

Q

Quick and Easy Blueberry Muffins	7

R

Roasted Brussels Sprouts with Orange and Garlic	61
Roasted Mushrooms with Garlic	58
Roasted Salmon Fillets	35
Rosemary Sweet Potato Veggie Hash	12
Rosemary-Garlic Shoestring Fries	55

S

Saucy Beef Fingers	49
Savory Beef and Pork Banger Meatloaf	42
Savory Garlic Steak Nuggets	50
Savory Mushroom and Barley Pilaf	66
Savory Mushroom and Gruyère Tarts	58
Savory Spinach & Swiss Mushroom Frittata	9
Sea Bass with Crispy Potato Scales and Caper Aïoli	35
Sirloin Steaks with Eggs	11
Smoky Chipotle Chicken Drumsticks	22
Snapper with Shallot and Tomato	34
Soft white cheese Stuffed Jalapeño Chillies Poppers	58
Spiced Air-Fried Pork Loin Ribs with Barbecue Glaze	46
Spiced Merguez-Style Chicken Meatballs	25
Spicy Air-Fried Chilli Prawns	32
Spicy Chicken Bites	52
Spicy Corn and Coriander Salad with Adobo Dressing	60
Spicy Firecracker Prawns	37
Spinach and Bacon Roll-ups	10
Steak Tips and Potatoes	15
Strawberry Pastry Rolls	71
Strawberry Toast	9
Stuffed Ricotta Potatoes with Herbs and Cheese	62
Swedish Meatloaf	45
Sweet and Spicy Blackened Tilapia	38
Sweet Potato Black Bean Burgers	67
Swordfish Skewers with Mediterranean Caponata	39

T

Teriyaki Cauliflower	68
Tex-Mex Salmon Bowl	37
Thanksgiving Turkey Breast	23
Thyme & Parsley Buttered Beef Fillet	47
Tomato and Bacon Zoodles	48
Tropical Chicken with Pineapple and Peach	26
Tuna Melt	34
Tuna Patties with Spicy Sriracha Sauce	39
Tuna Steaks with Olive Tapenade	33
Tuna with Herbs	36
Tuscan Herb-Crusted Veal Loin	44

V

Vietnamese Shaking Beef with Fresh Herb Salad	48

Z

Zesty Chicken and Avocado Fajitas	27
Zesty Lime-Pepper Steak Stir	49
Zesty Pepper-Stuffed Chicken Rolls	26
Zesty Pork Sliders with Red Cabbage Crunch	16

Printed in Great Britain
by Amazon